THE NIAGARA FRONTIER

its place in U.S. and Canadian history

THE NIAGARA FRONTIER

its place in U.S. and Canadian history

by

Robert Higgins

UPNEY EDITIONS

ISBN 0-9681403-0-0

UPNEY EDITIONS
19 Appalachian Crescent
Kitchener, Ontario
N2E 1A3 Canada

Canadian Cataloguing in Publication Data

Higgins, Robert, 1946—
      The Niagara Frontier: its place in U.S. and Canadian history

Includes bibliographical references and index.
ISBN 0-9681403-0-0

      1. Niagara River Region (N.Y. and Ont.)—
History. I. Title.

FC3095.N5H53 1996   971.3'38   C96-900814-7
F127.N6H53 1996

For Lynda

THE NIAGARA FRONTIER

Table of Contents

THE NIAGARA FRONTIER

Introduction

The passing of time is as inevitable as the rising and the setting of the sun, or perhaps, more aptly in this case, the steady flow of water over a waterfall. When we study the passage of time and try to make sense of events that have taken place in the past, we call it history. This then, is the history, albeit incomplete and condensed, of an area of land whose name is common to both the United States of America and Canada, and of a waterfall whose name is known throughout the world.

It was but two long lifetimes ago that events, perhaps unfathomable to us today, occurred along the Niagara Frontier. At the end of 1813, Buffalo, New York, was razed to the ground during an Indian attack and some of its inhabitants were slaughtered and scalped. And in 1814, at Hamilton, Ontario, eight men convicted of treason were punished in the most barbaric fashion. Not satisfied with death by hanging, the law of the time required that their

THE NIAGARA FRONTIER

heads be chopped off and exhibited as a grim warning to other would-be traitors. These are just two examples of events that occurred on the Niagara Frontier in relatively recent history—events that helped shape the Niagara of today and greatly influenced the histories of both Canada and the United States.

This book is an attempt to place before the reader, in as entertaining a manner as possible, a chronology of significant events on both sides of the Niagara Frontier, from the formation of the Falls to an oft forgotten invasion of Canada by Fenian forces in 1866. It is largely a military history, because that most accurately reflects the Frontier's tempestuous past. Niagara often provided the battleground for Indians fighting Indians, Indians fighting the white man, French fighting the British and their respective Indian allies, Americans fighting the British and its colony of Upper Canada, and even the Irish fighting the British!

For the purposes of this book, the Niagara Frontier is defined as being that territory adjacent to both sides of the Niagara River, extending as far east as the Genesee River on the U.S. side, and covering the northern shore of the Niagara Peninsula as far west as the Hamilton area, and from St. Catharines in the north to Port Colborne in the south, including that area around Fonthill known as the Short Hills, on the Canadian side.

One of the most famous places in the world, Niagara possesses a history to rival its beauty.

Robert Higgins
Hamilton, Ontario

THE NIAGARA FRONTIER

Niagara in North America

THE NIAGARA FRONTIER

Chapter 1
The Birth of the Falls

"Then with angry roar the legions bound along the opposing rock, until they reach the awful brink, where all surcharged with frantic fury, they leap bellowing down the fearful rocks thunder back the sullen echoes of thy voice, and shout God's power above the cloudy skies."

—James A. Garfield, 20th President of the United States, 1881, upon viewing Niagara Falls—

From two million or more years ago up until approximately 10,000 B.C., a length of time the geologists describe as the Pleistocene Epoch of the Quaternary Period, a glacier, some 1,000 metres (3,000 feet) thick and exerting a force of 904 tonnes per square metre (84 tons per square foot), blanketed the Earth from the Northern Polar Cap to as far south as Indiana. This glacier, named by geologists the Labrador Ice Sheet, we know today as the last Ice Age.

THE NIAGARA FRONTIER

Ice Age North America

Source: Historical Atlas of Canada (Kerr, 1975).

THE NIAGARA FRONTIER

Gradually, as the climate slowly moderated, the glacier-monster crept back towards its eventual Arctic home in an irregular, erratic fashion, scraping and scouring here, missing an area there. One of its prolonged visitations occurred in the Niagara area, where for a period of 25,000—35,000 years the combined weight and scouring action of the melting glacier created the Niagara River, extending from Lake Erie to a small shallow lake called Lake Tonawanda. Five small cataracts (at the present-day locations of Queenston-Lewiston, Lockport, Gasport, Medina and Holley, New York) provided outlets for Lake Tonawanda from the huge overflow from Lake Erie, caused by the meltwater from the receding glacier. However, a combination of soft soil and lower elevation resulted in the Queenston-Lewiston cataract becoming the sole outlet from Lake Tonawanda to Lake Ontario's ancestor, Lake Iroquois, which lay some 11 meters (35 feet) below Lake Tonawanda. These same soft underlying layers of shale and limestone, deposited during the Ordovician and Silurian periods some 505 to 408 million years ago, allowed further erosion to continue and turned the trickle into a torrent, eventually creating a cascade 11 meters (35 feet) high, with approximately one quarter of the volume of water that now flows over Niagara. The embryonic Niagara Falls were born!

With the passing of time, natural forces worked their magic on the Falls, increasing the power of its flow to carve, cut and sculpt the rock downstream into yet another masterpiece: the Niagara Gorge. The creation of the gorge took place over the next 12,000 years as the Falls retreated southwards 11 kilometers (7 miles) at the rate of about 1.1 metres (3.5 feet) per year from their birthplace at

THE NIAGARA FRONTIER

The Glaciers Retreat

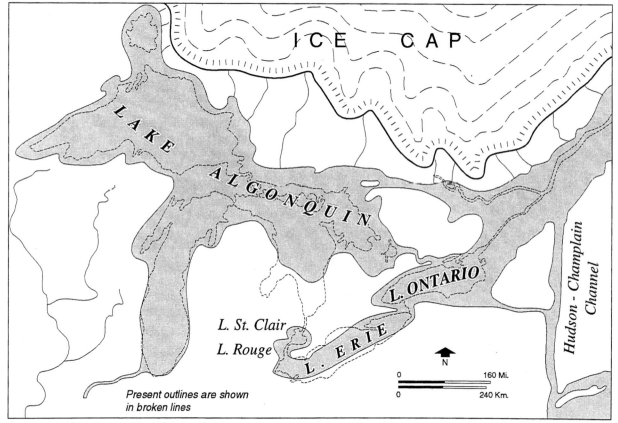

ICE CAP

LAKE ALGONQUIN

L. ONTARIO

L. ERIE

L. St. Clair
L. Rouge

Hudson - Champlain Channel

N

0   160 Mi.
0   240 Km.

*Present outlines are shown
in broken lines*

Source: Historical Atlas of Canada (Kerr, 1975).

Queenston-Lewiston to where they presently separate the cities of Niagara Falls, Ontario and Niagara Falls, New York. It is here, some 600 years ago, that geologists believe that Niagara split into two separate cataracts: the larger cataract would later become known as the Horseshoe Falls and the smaller waterfall the

THE NIAGARA FRONTIER

Recession of the Horseshoe Falls, 1378 - 1927

Source: Guide to the Geology of the Niagara Escarpment.

American Falls. Today there are three separate cascades at Niagara with the much smaller Luna Falls separating the two major cataracts.

Yet another natural source of fascination is the whirlpool, a large circular basin on the Canadian side of the river located between present-day Niagara Falls and Queenston. Here, the great volume of water discharged from the rapids upstream has scoured a deep basin in the soft sandstone. Water in the whirlpool basin normally circulates counterclockwise, although in times of low discharge it will circulate in the reverse direction. Water leaving the whirlpool continues its journey northwards to Lake Ontario.

THE NIAGARA FRONTIER

Lake Tonawanda and its Outlets

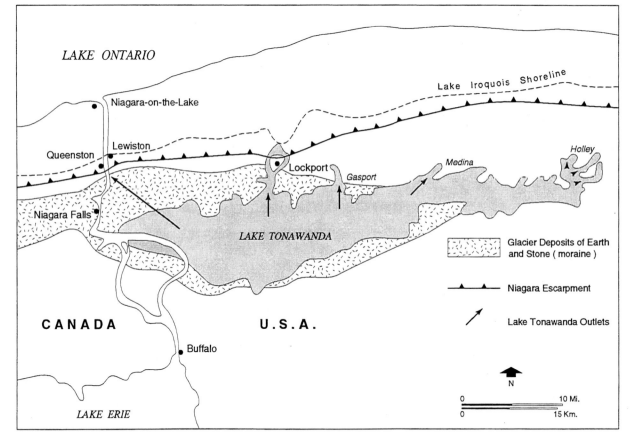

Source: Guide to the Geology of the Niagara Escarpment, Dr. Walter M. Tovell (Niagara Escarpment Commission, 1992).

Niagara Falls, its Gorge, and the Niagara River, were created by a process of dynamic geology, which still continues. Though native peoples of the area certainly knew of their existence, eons will pass before the explorer, Father Hennepin, announces the existence of the great cataract to the world in 1679.

THE NIAGARA FRONTIER

The Niagara Peninsula was, by its very nature, a barrier and an enormous natural obstacle to early wanderers upon the North American continent. A place of extraordinary beauty, mystery, myth, and promise, it became a stage for those players through history who were to tread upon its soil and sail upon its treacherous waters. As a political frontier it shaped the future of four nations, and great battles were fought there. French, British, American, Indian, Irish and Canadian blood was shed there, and heroes, traitors, and martyrs all played their respective parts.

The Niagara Frontier is a frontier forged both by the relentless forces of nature and by the steel and the bullets and the determination of man.

*"Here all the fury since the world was young
Is chanted on one tongue."*

—Wilson MacDonald, Niagara, 1926—

THE NIAGARA FRONTIER

THE NIAGARA FRONTIER

Chapter 2
The First Nation of Niagara

"When your time comes to die, be not like those whose hearts are filled with the fear of death, so when their time comes they weep and pray for a little more time to live their lives over again in a different way. Sing your death song, and die like a hero going home."

—*Tecumseh, Shawnee, ca. 1800*—

In about 20,000 B.C. Man departed Asia, crossing Beringia, a landmass stretching from Siberia to Alaska and the Northwest Territories, that formed when sea-levels became lower during an interglacial period. Thus began Man's long trek southwards along the western coast of North America, to become the first inhabitants of the New World. We do not know precisely when he moved inland, but by

THE NIAGARA FRONTIER

Beringia

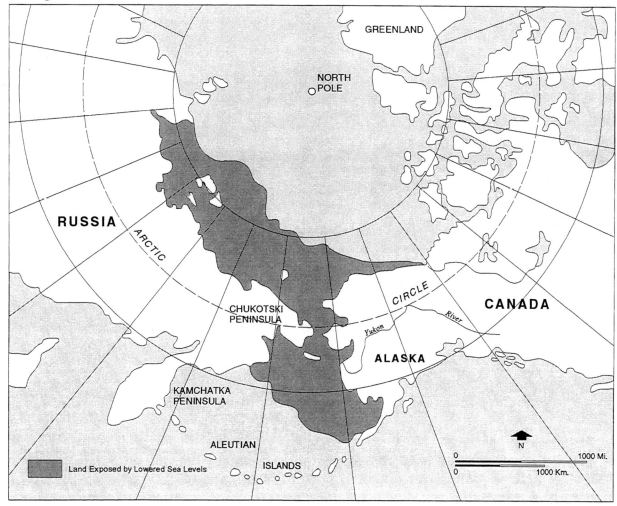

Source: Canadian Encyclepedia.

THE NIAGARA FRONTIER

1000 A.D., Algonquins, a nomadic hunting people, are known to have been living in the Niagara Frontier area. It is likely that by 1300 A.D. another people, the Iroquois, replaced the Algonquins, becoming the Frontier's new custodians. (Note: Because of scant evidence, we do not know whether earlier tribes migrated from the Niagara area in search of new food supplies or were conquered.)

In 1615 A.D. the great French explorer, Samuel de Champlain, recorded contact between Étienne Brûlé, a French explorer, and a large group of Indians that Champlain named *'La Nation Neutre'* or the Neutral Nation. Since they were not at war with either the neighbouring Huron to the west, or with the Senecas, who formed the largest tribe of the powerful Iroquois Confederacy to the east, the Neutral Nation, therefore, effectively served as a buffer between two traditionally hostile foes.

The Neutral Nation

In the first quarter of the seventeenth century, French missionaries estimated the population of the Neutral Nation at between 30,000 and 40,000, which was greater than either of that of the Huron—thought to number 25,000—or of the Iroquois Confederacy—estimated at approximately 15,000. By 1640, however, French missionaries had revised down their estimate of the Neutral population to only 12,000.

The Neutral, of Iroquois stock themselves, lived in about 20 or more villages dispersed throughout the Niagara Peninsula as far

THE NIAGARA FRONTIER

Distribution of Iroquoian Tribes in Lower Great Lakes

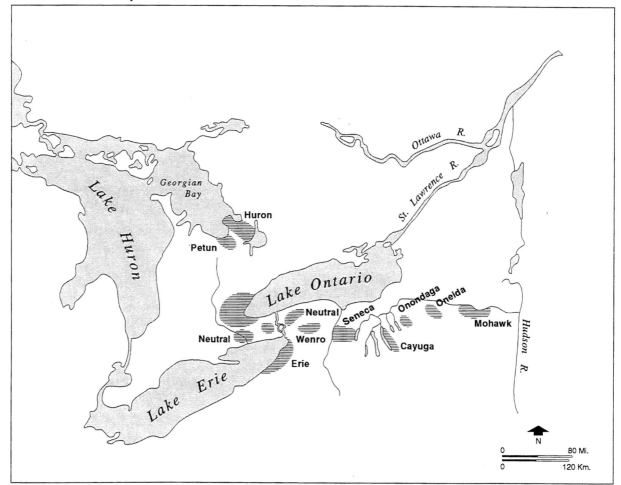

Source: The Grimsby Site: A Historic Neutral Cemetery, W.A. Kenyon, 1992.

THE NIAGARA FRONTIER

west as present-day London, Ontario, and as far east as the Genesee River in western New York State. Reports by missionaries indicate that eight of these villages were protected by palisades. The principal Neutral settlement was Ounonisaston, which was located near present-day Brantford, Ontario. Most of the Neutral villages were located in the Hamilton-Brantford area. Those Neutrals who lived along the Niagara River were known as 'Onguiaronon' (People of the Niagara).

The Neutral lived in bark-covered longhouses, each about 45 to 55 metres long (150 to 180 feet) and 10 to 15 metres wide (35 to 50 feet) with a central passage about three metres (10 feet) in width. In the hot summer months, they slept on shelves along the side of the lodge to avoid vermin, and during the long cold winter they slept inside on mats spread around fires in the centre of the floor. These lodges held anywhere from eight to 24 families.

The Neutral were primarily an agrarian people, raising crops of corn, beans, squash and pumpkins. To this basic diet they added fish and the meat from wildlife such as deer, elk, beaver, wild geese, cranes and turkey, which were all plentiful in the Niagara area at that time.

The Neutral were also a tall people, taller than the Huron, even taller than the French themselves. The males practised tattooing extensively. French Jesuits believed the Neutral lacked modesty, as the men rarely wore loin cloths during summer and the women covered themselves only from the waist to the knees. Other clothing, when worn, consisted of skirts, leggings, sleeves, moccasins,

THE NIAGARA FRONTIER

Tribal Territory and Archeological Sites

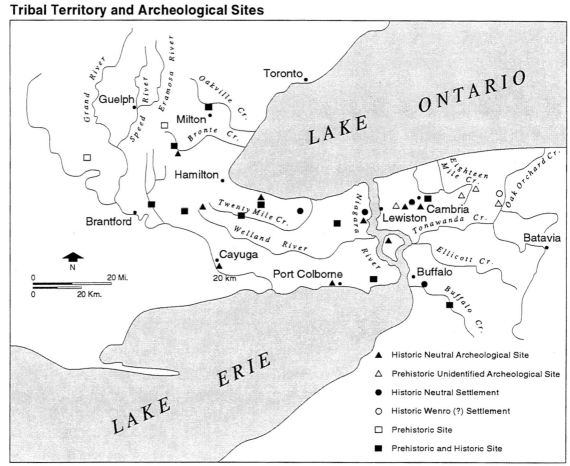

Source: *Handbook of North American Indians, Vol. 15 Bruce Trigger, (Ed.) 1978.*

THE NIAGARA FRONTIER

and in winter, fur robes. Sea shells from the Gulf of Mexico and beads from the Montreal area found in a Grimsby, Ontario burial site attest to the wealth of the Neutral and to the far-reaching extent of their trading empire.

The Neutral may have differed considerably from their Huron and Iroquois kin in terms of their political organization. Instead of one chief with authority over one tribe, the Neutral leader commanded all of his people. We have the name of a great leader handed down to us: Souharissen or Tsohahissen. It must also be said that we cannot be sure whether the Neutral people were in fact several villages of one nation, or a confederation of several separate tribes. All documented accounts of the Neutral were made during only three visits by the French: the first in 1615 by Brûlé, as recorded by Champlain, the second in 1626, by Father Joseph Daillon, and the third, in 1640/41, by Fathers Jérome Lalemant, Jean de Brébeuf and Joseph Chaumonot. Since none of these men is known to have been an ethnographer (those who systematically record and study human societies), we must regard as speculative, the record that they have left us.

Though the term Neutral may suggest that they were a peaceful people, it is misleading. Though at peace with the Huron and Iroquois, they frequently waged war against other tribes, especially the Mascouten, an Algonkian tribe in Michigan. Given the normal degree of care and attention that the Neutral gave to the burial of their own dead, the discovery of human bones, in 1897, at the bottom of a large bed of ashes at a Neutral campsite in East Flamboro, near Hamilton, suggests strongly to archaeologists that

THE NIAGARA FRONTIER

the Neutral practised cannibalism on their enemies.

The Death of a Nation

The Neutral, at the beginning of the seventeenth century, were a powerful people. They were wealthy, as is indicated by the materials found at their burial sites, and they were influential. Not only did they outnumber both the Huron and the Iroquois Confederacy, but they prospered in the role of buffer between these powerful and often warring neighbours. However, disaster struck in 1650 and 1651, when the Iroquois attacked and completely destroyed the Neutral both as a nation and as a cultural group.

One might ask: how could this happen so abruptly? There were several reasons. The first is that the Huron and Iroquois were traditional enemies and the demise of either one would have put the Neutral, living precariously between them, in jeopardy. But there was an even greater cause for the demise of the Neutral, and one that they shared with many other Indian nations throughout North America—the coming of the white man.

When the Iroquois received new formidable weapons in the form of muskets from the Dutch, they used them to attack their historic enemy, the Huron, destroying this nation in the year 1648. The Neutral's value as a buffer state between them effectively vanished. The lands of the Neutral are described in historical texts as being rich in beaver. Since beaver furs were one of the trade items most prized by Europeans, they were in great demand and

THE NIAGARA FRONTIER

in turn brought great wealth to those tribes that could deliver them. The Iroquois, who now wielded the strongest Indian confederacy (it endured until the American Revolution of 1776) and were in an expansionist frame of mind after defeating the Huron, first turned their attention towards the Neutral, and later the smaller tribes of the Wenro (closely related to the Neutral) and the Erie in Western New York and Pennsylvania. The fact that the Neutral had been greatly reduced in their numbers as a result of 'white man's' diseases, spread by the missionaries, and for which the Neutral had no natural immunity, must also be considered a major reason for their defeat. This would also explain the vast difference in population estimates: as high as 40,000 in 1626 by Daillon, and as low as 12,000 in 1640 by de Brébeuf and Chaumonot.

Today, Neutral blood still flows in the veins of the Iroquois and Wyandot peoples. Neutral survivors fled either west to form the Wyandot tribe, along with other homeless Huron (they too were fleeing the Iroquois and eventually settled in Oklahoma), or were assimilated into the Iroquois themselves. A map dated 1656 showing survivors of the nation living south of Lake Erie, is the last record of the Neutral as a unified group. After that the Neutral, who have given us one of the world's most famous names— Niagara— apparently ceased to be, and we are left with only the tantalizingly brief descriptions of them by French missionaries. Hopefully, new archaeological evidence of their existence may yet be found that will help fill an intellectual and emotional abyss that stretches back 350 years to the prophetic death song of a nation that died.

THE NIAGARA FRONTIER

Niagara

The Origin of a Name Known Around the World

Ongiarah, Ouinagarah and Ongniaraha are just a few of the many variations of Niagara that have been handed down to us. Since the native people known as the Neutral had inhabited the Niagara Frontier for perhaps three centuries before the French arrived on the scene, we can postulate that the French, in their day to day encounters with the Neutral, learned these names and in doing so modified them and absorbed them into their own language. In fact, a French map dated 1680 refers to a destroyed Neutral village situated close to the Niagara River as 'Niagagerega'.

If the name Niagara is indeed Neutral in origin, then it would be the only Neutral word to survive to today. Its meaning is said to be 'Thunder of the Waters'.

THE NIAGARA FRONTIER

The Niagara Frontier as a stage for human drama now fell quiet until the French realized its strategic importance in establishing its new colony of New France.

"What I offer you is to be while the water flows and the sun rises."

—Alexander Morris,
during Indian treaty negotiations, 1873—

THE NIAGARA FRONTIER

THE NIAGARA FRONTIER

Chapter 3
Niagara's French Connection

"The savages did not become French, but the French became savages."

—Pierre-François-Xavier de Charlevoix: History and General Description of New France, published 1744—

With the dispersal of the Neutral Nation, the Iroquois, *"The Romans of the West"*, reigned supreme. French activity lay dormant until awakened by a new spirit of expansionism entering the late 1660s. The French explorers, Pierre Esprit Radisson and his brother-in-law, Medard Chouart, better known by his assumed title of Groseilliers,

THE NIAGARA FRONTIER

La Salle
Courtesy of National Archives of Canada
C-7802

THE NIAGARA FRONTIER

were approaching the Mississippi River; the French were building Forts St. Jean and Chambly along the Richelieu River, between Lake Champlain and the St. Lawrence River; and Quebec (New France) itself was growing.

The Arrival of La Salle

With the advent of the year 1669, Robert Cavelier de La Salle, visited the Niagara Frontier to establish friendly relations with the Seneca.

La Salle, born in Rouen, France, in 1643, into a wealthy family, had studied to become a missionary but his energy and drive proved to be too much for either him or his superiors to handle. The dangers and uncertainties of life in the New World tempted his brave, stout heart, and he departed for La Nouvelle-France in 1666, at the age of 23.

At this time the French still moved their goods and conducted their efforts to colonize the Mississippi through Huronia, the land beside Georgian Bay (eastern Lake Huron) that had been occupied by the Huron Indians in Ontario. With the supremacy of the Iroquois Confederacy, the Niagara Frontier now took on a strategic significance for the French if they were to protect their trade routes to the riches of the west. The French dealt peacefully with the Iroquois, as was their official policy.

La Salle returned to France to secure permission to explore and colonize the lands along the Mississippi River, and planned to use fur to pay for the new venture. Successful in his mission, he returned to

THE NIAGARA FRONTIER

The Building of La Salle's Griffon
from Louis Hennepin's "Nouvelle Découverte d'un trés grand pays situé dans l'Amérique", Utrecht, 1697. The artist is an unknown to us as Niagara was to the artist, given the fanciful mountains and tropical trees. Courtesy: National Archives of Canada/C-1225.

THE NIAGARA FRONTIER

Fort Frontenac (Kingston, Ontario) in 1677 to implement this new policy. He began to plan the construction of two ships, one to sail on Lake Ontario and one for Lake Erie, and looked to establish a strategic location on the Niagara Frontier to act as a protective link between New France and the Mississippi. Later he met with his expedition on the east bank of the northern mouth of the Niagara River where he built Fort Conti. The fort was located at the northern end of the Indian portage, a trail used by them to circumvent the stretch of the Niagara River that was not navigable. La Salle was able to do this because he had the permission of the Iroquois, made possible by the diplomatic efforts of Father Louis Hennepin.

At the southern terminus of the Indian portage, at the mouth of Cayuga Creek, he built *"Le Griffon"* - the *Griffon* - the first sailing ship to navigate the Great Lakes above Niagara Falls. Using this ship, La Salle planned to supply France's intended new colonies along the length of the Mississippi, and to return to Niagara loaded with furs. La Salle's plans for the *Griffon* were not to be realized however, for after completing her first voyage to present-day Green Bay, Wisconsin, in 1679, she foundered on her return to Niagara during a storm, with the loss of the crew of five men. In 1955 the remains of a wreck, thought to resemble the *Griffon* in many ways, were found in a sheltered cove on Russell Island in Georgian Bay, just north of the Bruce Peninsula. For a time it appeared that the mystery of La Salle's *Griffon* was solved, but in 1980 a three year Ontario government investigation concluded that the remains of the vessel were those of a mid 19th century ship modeled after a craft known as the 'Collingwood Skiff'.

If the *Griffon* had survived to supply the French outposts along the

THE NIAGARA FRONTIER

Niagara Falls
by Father Louis Hennepin
Courtesy of the Buffalo and Erie County Historical Society, #20291-A

THE NIAGARA FRONTIER

Mississippi as La Salle had intended, then certainly France would have been in a vastly stronger position in the New World. Her loss, however, while not crippling to French efforts in the New World, was far from insignificant either, since La Salle was denied the opportunity to use the *Griffon* to bring French commodities to the Iroquois at a cheaper price than could the English.

The French Pull Back

Meanwhile, French policy towards the Iroquois was changing for the worse. When Compte de Louis de Buade Frontenac, governor of New France, was recalled to France, that nation's benign dealings with the Iroquois come to an abrupt end. The new governor, the Marquis de Denonville, attacked and destroyed much of the Seneca homeland (part of the Iroquois Confederacy) during the summer of 1687. Although few Indian lives were lost, the Seneca and Iroquois were understandably outraged over these attacks. Denonville retreated to the mouth of the Niagara River at Lake Ontario where he built a fort with two large guns and several cabins. After providing a garrison for the fort, Denonville returned to Montreal for supplies. The Iroquois began to kill any Frenchmen they found hunting outside of the fort, culminating with the death of the garrison commander. A new commander, Captain Raymond Desbergères began to rebuild Fort Conti, however, in September, 1688, he received orders to abandon the structure. He complied, but not before first destroying the fort to prevent it falling into enemy hands. Once again the Niagara Frontier belonged to the Indians, if only for a short time.

THE NIAGARA FRONTIER

The French and the Niagara Frontier, 1759

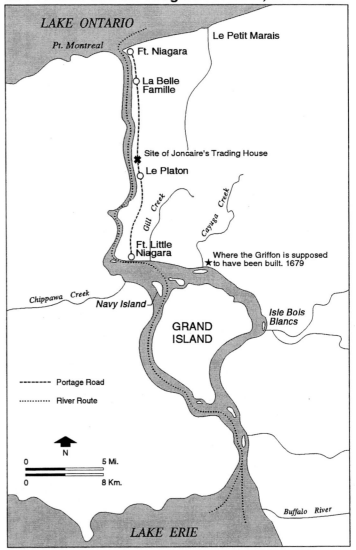

Source: George A. Bevan: The Role of the Niagara Frontier in Canadian Military History (A Study of Historical Geography). Thesis: McMaster 1948.

THE NIAGARA FRONTIER

The Return of Frontenac

In 1689, Frontenac returned from France with a sword in his right hand and a torch in his left. His intention was to subdue the warring Iroquois whose homes lay to the east of the Niagara Frontier. He was so successful that it took the Iroquois 50 years to recover their former position and strength.

The quotation at the beginning of this chapter reflects the failed policy of the French towards building and keeping their empire in the New World. In truth it was not so much that the policy itself failed but that it suffered from a fundamental weakness in its execution. Instead of following the policy set out by the King of France and France's Colonial Office—one of confining settlements with direct maritime access to France, and building those communities in places where they could be protected—Frontenac and other administrators of New France sought the potential wealth that the fur trade could bring to France (and themselves) with the result that French power was diluted and a strain was put on her resources in the new world.

In 1719, the French received permission from the Seneca to build an outpost that they named 'Magazin Royal' at the northern end of the Indian portage trail where, earlier, La Salle had built a storehouse. The French were able to do this, despite hostilities, because of the influence of a Frenchman, Chabert de Joncaire, who lived with the Seneca and was one of the leaders of the Iroquois. Magazin Royal prospered. French ships deposited wares from Fort Frontenac and departed Niagara loaded with furs. Missionaries, explorers, and Seneca warriors constantly came and went. The

THE NIAGARA FRONTIER

The Niagara Frontier in its Great Lakes Setting

Source: The Role of the Niagara Frontier in Canadian Military History (A Study in Historical Geography) George A. Bevan, Thesis (Mac) 1948.

French had realized their goal and now possessed a strong foothold on the Niagara River not only to foster and protect their interests in the fur trade, but to maintain their supremacy in the region, and to provide that vital link that allowed them to take control of the upper Great Lakes, the Mississippi, and the Ohio Valley. The time for them to construct a genuine fortress on the Frontier had arrived. A brick building,which was actually a self-contained fort capable of withstanding an Indian attack, was built in 1725 and still stands today—the oldest building on the Niagara Frontier.

THE NIAGARA FRONTIER

Later known as 'The Castle', its innocuous appearance was meant to dispel any alarm among the Indians.

Meanwhile, the British colonies continued to grow and expand westwards, eventually becoming a menace to the French fur trade. The fact was not lost on the Government of New France, which realized the vulnerability of its principal source of wealth. Quickly a string of new forts was added to the established forts at Quebec, Frontenac (Kingston), and Niagara. They included Fort Presqu' Isle at Erie, Pennsylvania, Fort Le Boeuf at Watertown, Pennsylvania, Fort Machault at Franklin, Pennsylvania, and Fort Duquesne at Pittsburgh, Pennsylvania. These forts were all in place by 1754.

To the French, Fort Niagara was the vital link that ensured the flow of furs from the west to the Great Lakes, thence to Niagara, and on to Quebec, for ultimate export to France.

The British were not slow to react to this proliferation of French forts. They sent a small force, led by future American president George Washington, to Fort Duquesne, where he was to request the French to leave. The French replied with their muskets—the British promptly fled—and The Seven Years' War between France and Britain began.

The Seven Years' War

This major conflict began with Washington's defeat on 3 July, 1754, although war was not formally declared until 17 May, 1756.

THE NIAGARA FRONTIER

The Castle at Fort Niagara
Oldest building on the Frontier
Photo by the author

THE NIAGARA FRONTIER

Niagara: The Strategic Key to Greater New France

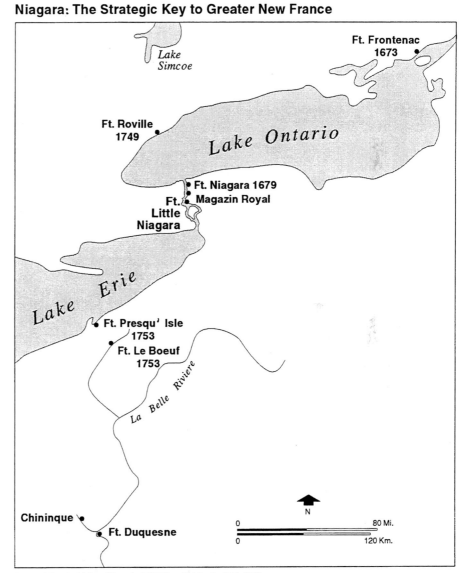

Source: Historical Atlas of Canada, DGG Kerr, 3rd Revised Ed, 1975.

THE NIAGARA FRONTIER

A brief overview of the events occurring outside of the Niagara Frontier is now in order. The British commander, General Braddock, suffered a major defeat (and lost his life) when his force was ambushed by the French and their Indian allies as they approached Fort Duquesne. The British met with success at Fort Oswego on Lake Ontario as well as in the Lake Champlain region. In the east they captured Fort Beauséjour on 16 June, 1755. Both the French and the British began building new forts in the Lake Champlain region. Montcalm, the new French commander-in-chief, recaptured and then destroyed Fort Oswego. He also captured the new British fort, Fort William Henry, which stood at the southern extremity of Lake George (south of Lake Champlain in upper New York state), on 9 August, 1757. In 1758 the French repulsed the British at Fort Carillon, near Lake Champlain, but the great French fortress of Louisbourg, on Cape Breton Island, fell to the British, as did Forts Frontenac and Duquesne.

The Siege of Fort Niagara

The Niagara Frontier remained comparatively peaceful during the years 1755 to 1759. The French refortified Fort Niagara, fully realizing its importance in retaining hold of their tenuous empire in the west. But the French still inconceivably underestimated the British threat to the Niagara region, leaving Fort Niagara, which was capable of housing 1,000 men, with a meagre garrison of fewer than 500 men.

On 1 July 1759, British commander, General John Prideaux, landed at Le Petit Marais, about eight kilometers (five miles) east of

THE NIAGARA FRONTIER

Fort Niagara, with 2,200 enlisted men and 700 Iroquois warriors. From there the British force marched to besiege Fort Niagara. General Prideaux died during the siege and Sir William Johnson took command. French reinforcements, stationed on Navy Island, received orders to advance to Fort Niagara, but were ambushed by the British at La Belle Famille, at present-day Youngstown, New York. Under a truce, the French commanding officer at Niagara, Captain François Pouchot, ordered one of his officers to review the battle site at La Belle Famille, and upon receiving his officer's report, surrendered to the British on the night of 24 July, 1759. The loss of Fort Niagara coincided with the taking of Quebec by British forces and was the beginning of the end of French rule in the New World. France formally capitulated to Britain on 8 September, 1760.

The British Threat to America

It was now France's turn to depart Niagara's stage. With the French threat removed, the American colonies began to view Britain as more of a tyrant than a protector. And with battle hardened veterans from The Seven Years' War to draw upon, the colonies would successfully gain their independence from Britain in the American Revolution of 1776. This hostility changed the face of Niagara once again, bringing an influx of American colonialists with names like Butler and Secord. They were United Empire Loyalists—refugees in the most basic sense—fleeing persecution in their newly formed nation because of their allegiance to Britain and the King. The United States and Britain were about

THE NIAGARA FRONTIER

to take centre stage to enact Niagara's most dramatic episode: The War of 1812.

"The blood-red blossom of war
with a heart of fire"

—Alfred, Lord Tennyson,
1809-1892—

THE NIAGARA FRONTIER

Chapter 4

The Second War of Independence

" Coming to the house at Chippawa, I found Thomas Poe lying on a blanket. He reached his hand to me and told me that he was mortally wounded, and that he had but a few moments to live, and told me he wished to be buried on the American side of the river... Carrying him nearly a mile across the plain, in the middle of 26 July, appeared to exhaust what little strength he had left... He shook hands with me for the last time. He said to me in a weak voice: 'Alexander, you will never see me again in this world.' He expired in a few minutes."

—Private Alexander McMullen, Col. Fenton's Regiment Pennsylvania Volunteers. (After the Battle of Lundy's Lane)—

THE NIAGARA FRONTIER

Prelude to War on the Frontier

In 1764, the British strengthened Fort Niagara and built Fort Schlosser, at the southern terminus of the old portage on the east side of the Niagara River, and Fort Erie, on the west bank to guard the mouth of the Niagara River at Lake Erie.

It was a comparatively quiet period in Niagara's history with one notable exception. On 14 September 1763 about 500 Seneca warriors ambushed a British wagon train at a gulch known as the Devil's Hole, along the east bank of the river, between present-day Niagara Falls, New York and the Robert Moses Power Plant. Men, wagons, horses and oxen were thrown into the gorge. Eighty scalped bodies were found later with only three men escaping the slaughter. The three survivors warned troops at Lewiston, who set out to engage the Seneca, but were themselves ambushed. Only eight of the British troops survived.

This incident was inspired in part by Pontiac, the Ottawa Chieftain, who organized and led general uprisings against the English. But the main reason was retaliation against the British for replacing the Seneca with their own men, as carriers of goods along the portage. Under the French it had been a very profitable venture for the Seneca. The commemorative marker now erected at the site bills this massacre as America's first labor action. The attack eventually worked against the Seneca, however, as they had to plea for forgiveness from Sir William Johnson, the British commander, whose forces had captured Fort Niagara from the French, or else face his

THE NIAGARA FRONTIER

powerful army. Johnson agreed to forgive the Seneca, providing that they cede lands along both sides of the Niagara River. The once all-powerful Iroquois Confederation was literally losing ground.

The War of Independence

In the years to come animosity towards Britain increased, and the ideals of freedom and personal liberty took root in the American colonies. *"No taxation without representation"* was the slogan that united the 13 Colonies against Britain, which was in turn attempting to raise taxes in the colonies to fund their defense. Britain made no concessions to the colonies. With battle hardened veterans from The Seven Years' War to draw upon, the colonies were well prepared to fight for their independence from Britain, and The War of Independence—The *first* War of Independence—ensued.

The United Empire Loyalists

The Frontier saw little direct military action during these hostilities although Fort Niagara did serve as a base from which British supporters and Indians conducted guerrilla-type warfare against the rebellious colonies.

The great change that took place on the Frontier was not military; it was social and political. Citizens of the 13 colonies still loyal to the British crown, who refused to take the Oath of Allegiance to the President, fled their homeland either voluntarily or were forced out by the newly formed state governments and republican bent

THE NIAGARA FRONTIER

citizens. The means of expulsion and coercion included: personal exile, property seizures, loss of business, imprisonment, holding families hostage, and demeaning punishments like tar and feathering. Death and murder do not appear to have been extensively practised by the Revolutionaries against the Loyalists.

Fort Niagara provided sanctuary for about 6,000 of those colonialists who remained loyal to Britain, and many of them formed military units to combat the rebellious colonies. Butler's Rangers were one of these units. Today we call them 'United Empire Loyalists' and these refugees, fleeing America for the safety of a new land, would form the nucleus of Upper Canada society during the 1770s and 80s.

A New Capital—Niagara-on-the-Lake

The 13 Colonies ultimately defeated Britain in the War of Independence and, in 1783, the Treaty of Versailles required Britain to cede Forts Niagara and Schlosser to the newly-formed United States of America. It was not until 1796, however, that American troops actually took possession of those forts. During this time the British garrison and the Loyalists began an orderly settlement on the west side of the Niagara River, building a new town opposite Fort Niagara as the capital of the new region. Naming the town Newark, it became the site of the first meeting of parliament in 1791 in what was to become the nation of Canada. Newark would also be known by other names, such as Butlerbury, Butlersburg, Niagara, and West Niagara. We know it today as Niagara-on-the-Lake. Its glory was shortlived because of its prox-

THE NIAGARA FRONTIER

imity to the guns of Fort Niagara and the capital was soon shifted to York (now Toronto and also founded by Simcoe). In 1796, Simcoe built Fort George to offset the advantage that the Americans enjoyed with Fort Niagara and the two forts warily faced each other across the Niagara River.

The Arrival of Isaac Brock

New roads were built, and a new portage on the Canadian side of the Niagara River took form, from Queenston to Chippawa. The British built Fort Drummond at the northern terminus and Fort Chippawa at the southern terminus to protect this strategic route. Butler's Barracks were built at Newark to relieve the overcrowding at Fort George. And, in 1802, Colonel Isaac Brock arrived from England to assume responsibility for the protection of Upper Canada.

Born on Guernsey (one of Britain's Channel Islands), on 6 October, 1769, most of Brock's life was devoted to soldiering. He was an officer by the age of 15, served with distinction at the Battles of Egmont-op-Zee in The Netherlands in 1799, and took part in a naval battle at Copenhagen.

On the eastern side of the Niagara River the scattered semblance of civilized settlement began to take root in a number of places. At the hamlets of Youngstown and Eighteen Mile Creek; at Lewiston, which boasted a Centre for Navigation and a Customs House by the time the War of 1812 commenced; at the village of Manchester (now Niagara Falls, New York); and at the village of Black Rock,

THE NIAGARA FRONTIER

Isaac Brock
Courtesy: National Archives of Canada/C-36181

THE NIAGARA FRONTIER

which had the Frontier's best harbor on the eastern bank of the river. Buffalo, the principal American town on the Niagara Frontier, then had a population of about 600. Incidentally, Buffalo likely takes its name from a waterway in the area that was well known to early explorers as a place where they could find shelter and rest. The French name given to the creek, *La Rivière des Boeufs,* also appears as *Rivière des Bufles* on a French map dated 1785. Anglicized, the name became Buffalo Creek.

Tensions Escalate

Two similar but separate nascent societies were now forming along the Niagara Frontier. On the east side, the newest nation on the map, the United States of America, republican and individualistic, and on the west side, the British colony of Upper Canada, monarchical and more socially structured, whose birth into nationhood still lay some seventy years in the future. Blood was the common denominator between these two similar yet polarized societies; blood begot through kinship, blood spilled during the American Revolution; and the blood yet to be spilled during the war that inevitably was to come. Tensions between Britain and the United States continued to escalate during the first decade of the new century. The political courses that each nation had charted put both on a deadly collision course that became the War of 1812.

The Causes of the War of 1812

Britain and the United States were not on good terms. The passions, distrust and bitterness created by the *first* War of

THE NIAGARA FRONTIER

Independence were still alive and thriving in the hearts of those who lived on both sides of the Niagara River. Loyalties were still questionable. General Brock was convinced that his 49th Regiment was the only genuine military force in Upper Canada, since he regarded the Canadian militia as neither effective nor trustworthy.

The threat posed by Napoleon in Europe further exacerbated Anglo-American relations. With their superior navy, the British enacted a blockade around the European mainland to weaken the French. This act legitimized, in their view, the boarding and searching of neutral ships, including those of the United States. Britain also began impressing sailors on American ships whom she believed had deserted the British navy. Such actions infuriated the American Government. These then were the explicit causes of the war. The implicit cause was that the United States believed that Canada would be an easy conquest; after all, Britain had its hands full in Europe with Napoleon, and many of the inhabitants of Canada were believed to still sympathize with the United States. In the American Congress, the Hawks—those elected representatives who favoured war, led by Henry Clay, the senator from Kentucky—won out and war was declared on Britain and Her Dependencies on 18 June, 1812.

The War Begins

Several major battles of the War of 1812 occurred on the Niagara Frontier. At the start of the war the British captured Fort Michilimackinac in the north before the American soldiers garrisoned there were even aware that a state of war existed between

THE NIAGARA FRONTIER

The Niagara Theatre

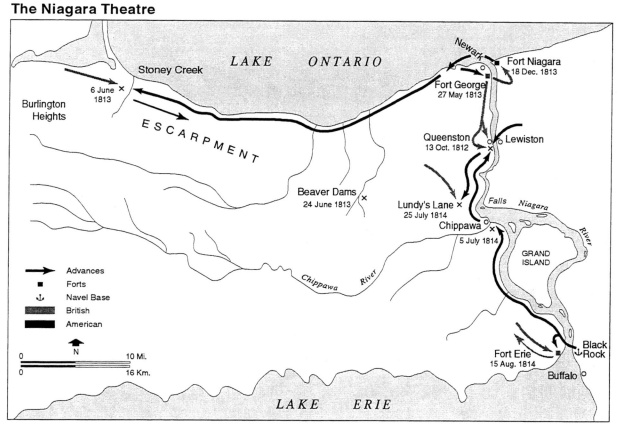

Source: Historical Atlas of Canada, D.G.G. Kerr, 3rd. Revised Ed., 1975.

THE NIAGARA FRONTIER

Britain and the United States. The attack, ordered by Brock, was bloodless.

William Hull, a hero of the American Revolution, and governor of the Michigan territory, led a large army to Fort Detroit in order to invade Canada but surrendered there to General Brock. Fear of slaughter by Indian warriors led by the great Shawnee chief, Tecumseh, coupled with the dashing and bold military manoeuvres of Brock, and the timidity shown by Hull, resulted in another bloodless victory—as brilliant for the British as it was ignominious for the Americans.

The Battle of Queenston Heights

The action swung now to the Frontier where the Americans amassed an army of regulars and militiamen under the leadership of Major General Stephen Van Rensselaer. His targets were Fort George and Queenston, but his counterpart at Fort Schlosser, General Alexander Smyth, refused to cooperate and Van Rensselaer decided to take only Queenston, the town at the northern end of the portage on the west side of the river.

On 13 October, 1812, after much difficulty caused by poor planning and organization and a lack of cooperation between the American regular and militia forces, the Americans managed to land on the west side of the river, at Queenston. The Americans scaled Queenston Heights by way of an old Indian path, attacking from the rear the Redan Battery, a lone British gun emplacement facing the American side. Brock, at Fort George, heard the gun fire

THE NIAGARA FRONTIER

and immediately departed for the battle site. Once there he ordered the gun spiked then returned to Queenston to ready his troops for a head-on assault of the American position. The two head-on assaults that followed, resulted in both Brock's death and that of his aide-de-camp, Lieutenant Colonel John Macdonell.

Writers of history sometimes accuse Brock of foolhardiness in ordering a direct assault upon the American position. It might well have been, but it should also be pointed out that it was by no means uncommon for a commander to be killed or wounded in action, given the type of warfare practised at that time. Van Rensselaer, too, was wounded at Queenston Heights; Wolfe and Montcalm both died at Quebec in 1759; Tecumseh died at the Battle of the Thames in 1813; four American leaders were wounded at Lundy's Lane in 1814; and Braddock, the English commander, died after being attacked by the French near Fort Duquesne in 1755. It was the nature of warfare during this period of history, fought at close quarters, without the benefit of technical communications or the protection afforded by distance, that commanders were almost as exposed to the immediate dangers of the battlefield as were the fighting troops. With black powder gunsmoke drifting in thick clouds across the battlefield, a commander could not afford to be far from his troops.

Following the death of Brock, Major General Roger Sheaffe, Brock's Second-in-Command, assumed leadership of the British forces. By leading his troops from Fort George to Queenston, thence to St. Davids, where he turned eastwards, he was able to circle behind the Americans and stage a surprise attack, overwhelming their left

THE NIAGARA FRONTIER

A Private's Life

A Private in the British regular army during the War of 1812 would have been accustomed to:

1. Wearing a leather collar (as would his American counterpart) to prevent him from becoming distracted in battle by the sight of fallen comrades.

2. Carrying 60 lbs (27 kg) of gear, much of it in a haversack with a wooden frame that would cut into his back on long marches.

3. Receiving pay of one shilling per day (about 10 cents today) before costs were deducted for food, medicine, etc.

4. Punishment of up to 300 whiplashes for behaviour contrary to regulations.

5. Drills and more drills, interspersed only by periods of unmitigated boredom.

6. Cooking and eating his own meals twice a day, early in the morning and at noon.

7. Consuming rum instead of contaminated water. The U.S. Army favoured Whiskey.

8. Being drunk much of the time (see #7), resulting in receiving punishment (i.e. lashes) for misconduct.

THE NIAGARA FRONTIER

flank and leaving them with their backs to the river and with no escape. It was Lieutenant Colonel Winfield Scott, a most durable soldier, about whom more will be said, who formally surrendered to the British.

Thus this second invasion of Canada ended with a pyrrhic victory for the British; pyrrhic because of the death of Brock. While Brock had been alive, the British government had found it difficult to find a hat large enough to fit his huge head (in fact, one was on order at the time of the battle). And with his death the British found it impossible to fill Brock's boots as well, since no replacement of his stature existed.

The Americans, meanwhile, attempted to advance to Montreal at the end of 1812, but instead withdrew. General Dearborn, with the assistance of the American navy, commanded by Captain Isaac Chauncey, attacked and burned York on 27 April, 1813. American forces also captured Newark and Fort George exactly one month later, forcing the British to retreat to Burlington Heights.

The Battle of Stoney Creek

On 6 June, 1813, under Brigadier General John Vincent, the British staged a night assault against the Americans, attacking from an unprotected gully at Stoney Creek, near present-day Hamilton, Ontario. Although the attack surprised the Americans, they fought back furiously. Soon the battle became confusing and chaotic because of the darkness, and friends were mistaken for foes. The British captured two American generals and four field

THE NIAGARA FRONTIER

guns. The American force retreated to Forty Mile Creek, near present-day Grimsby, Ontario.

There, on 7 June, 1813, the day after the Battle of Stoney Creek, units of the British Royal Navy, under the command of Sir James Yeo, commenced a bombardment of the American camp. Sixteen unguarded American boatloads of supplies from Fort Niagara were either captured or destroyed. It is at that point in the hostilities that the Americans decided to withdraw to Fort George, and another planned invasion of Upper Canada was thwarted.

Forcing their advantage, the British advanced towards the east with a split force to engage the Americans: those under the command of Major Peter De Haren marched against Fort George, while those commanded by Lieutenant James Fitzgibbon were to take Fort Erie. At the same time about 500 American troops under the command of Lieutenant Colonel Charles G. Boerstler were marching from Fort George to Queenston to stop Fitzgibbon from harassing the American line along the western Portage Road. Boerstler's target was Fitzgibbon's outpost at DeCew House, south of present-day St. Catharines. In the battle that followed, a legend was born.

Laura Secord

The Americans, under Captain Cyrenius Chapin, made plans to attack the Fitzgibbon force. Legend has it that these plans were made at the home of James and Laura Secord, formerly from Massachusetts. Whilst preparing the American officers' meal, which they had commandeered, Laura Secord overheard their

THE NIAGARA FRONTIER

plans to attack Fitzgibbon. Her husband, James, was still recovering from the wounds he had received at Queenston Heights, so Laura decided that she must attempt to warn the British of the impending attack.

Laura left her home at Queenston and, as a feint, walked to St. Davids for the apparent purpose of visiting her ill half brother. Laura's niece, Elizabeth, accompanied her for part of the journey but collapsed due to exhaustion. Laura continued on along Twelve Mile Creek which flows beside the DeCew House, and 30 kilometres (18 miles) later, arrived exhausted and hungry at an Indian encampment. The Indian chief took Laura to Fitzgibbon where she disclosed the American plans.

On 24 June 1813, Fitzgibbon, with 50 regulars and about 150 Cognawaga Indians, ambushed the American force on the Beaver Dams Trail at present-day Thorold, Ontario. Rather, it was the 150 Cognawaga under fur trader, François Dominique Ducharme, who attacked and defeated the Americans. Fitzgibbon only intervened to prevent a massacre and the scalping of Americans.

The Legend of Laura Secord is well-known today, and most certainly the story has been well embellished. But it is true that Laura Secord learned of the American plans, and that she did in fact warn Fitzgibbon of the impending attack. Fitzgibbon himself testified as such, and for her brave act Laura Secord was formally recognized by the British Government, receiving £100 in 1860 from the Prince of Wales. The long lapse of time between the end of the War of 1812 and official recognition for the part she had played was due,

THE NIAGARA FRONTIER

Map of Laura Secord's Walk

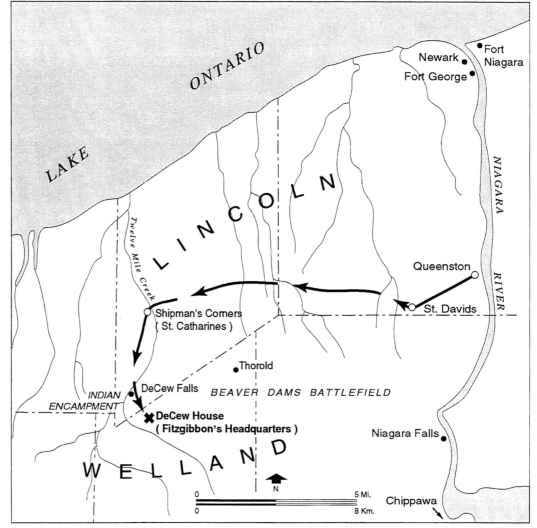

Source: Laura Secord by John Bassett, Fitzhenry and Whiteside Ltd., Roy Petrie Toronto, 1974, 1981.

THE NIAGARA FRONTIER

not to neglect or indifference on the part of the government (though her act did require a good deal of confirmation), but was rather one of protecting the Secord family from any backlash by Upper Canada's more republican leaning citizens.

Newark Burns

In July, after Beaver Dams, the British advanced to Fort George, then turned south towards Fort Erie in a cleanup type operation. On 5 July 1813, they attacked and destroyed Fort Schlosser on the east side, and on 11 July destroyed Black Rock. Virtually all remaining American solders withdrew to Fort George and Newark. Brigadier General George McClure, in charge of the American forces at Newark, believed the American position was now untenable on the west side of the Niagara Frontier. After ordering the complete destruction of Newark by fire, an act strongly influenced by Joseph Willcocks, a former Loyalist who turned traitor and was now an officer in the American Army, McClure and his troops evacuated the town. All buildings except some churches and one house were burned to the ground.

The Capture of Fort Niagara

The British immediately retaliated. Under Colonel John Murray, they readied themselves to storm Fort Niagara on 18 December 1813. After first bayonetting the pickets, they proceeded to the main gate, which they found open, and entered the fort. Here the Americans put up fierce resistance resulting in about 11 British casualties, including the death of Colonel Murray. Finally, the

THE NIAGARA FRONTIER

British prevailed, and several hundred prisoners were taken. One American account of the capture of Fort Niagara portrayed the British as slaughtering about 80 prisoners, many of them hospital patients. Another account described the capture as occurring *'without a shot being fired'*, which might be true as the British used the bayonet extensively so as to inflict an intentionally painful death upon the American defenders. Fort Niagara remained in British hands until peace prevailed in 1815.

The Destruction Continues

The British now turned their attention towards the rest of the Niagara Frontier on the American side of the river: Youngstown, then a hamlet, was completely destroyed by fire, as were Eighteen Mile Creek, Lewiston, and Manchester (now Niagara Falls, New York.). Fort Schlosser was burned, as were houses at Tonawanda Creek, LaSalle, Black Rock and Buffalo. American officials estimated a loss of 380 buildings on the Frontier. Unlike the destruction of Newark where there was no loss of human life, a number of American inhabitants did lose their lives in the reprisal fires that followed. American officials cited the deaths of Mrs. Lovejoy of Buffalo, the massacre of two large families at Black Rock, and other reprisals at Youngstown and Fort Niagara. The inhabitants of those communities were forced to flee and became refugees until the spring of 1814 when most returned.

In the other theatres of the war, the British continued to control the western front until 10 September, 1813, when the American naval commander, Commodore Oliver Hazard Perry, defeated the British

THE NIAGARA FRONTIER

at Put-In-Bay, at the western end of Lake Erie. This effectively put the American forces in control of the lake and with the advantage that this gave them they went on to enjoy more land victories.

The War's Final Year

In the early months of 1814, American forces controlled Lake Erie and Detroit and were growing in strength along the Niagara Frontier under Major General Jacob Brown. Lieutenant General Gordon Drummond, then the commander of British forces in Upper Canada, built Fort Mississauga upon the ruins of Newark. Along with Forts Niagara and George, a protective triangle was formed at the northern mouth of the Niagara River.

In July of that year a well seasoned American force, under Major General Brown, mounted yet another invasion of Canada and, on 3 July, defeated the British garrison at Fort Erie before moving on to Chippawa.

On 5 July, 1814, the Americans came upon a British force at Chippawa, under the command of Major General Phineas Riall. The American militia, commanded by Brigadier General Peter B. Porter, initially retreated from the advancing British. Riall ordered a frontal attack but the British were beaten back by accurate American artillery fire, disciplined veteran foot solders, and decisive leadership.

One of those decisive leaders was Winfield Scott, who earlier had surrendered to the British at Queenston Heights and who was sub-

THE NIAGARA FRONTIER

sequently pardoned on condition that he not fight again against the British. Knowing that if he were ever captured by the British he would likely face a firing squad, Scott, a huge, durable, bold and brave Virginian, survived the War of 1812 and went on to other battles. His forces captured Mexico City in 1847 and he continued to serve his country on the Chiefs of Staff in Washington until the outbreak of the American Civil War.

Retreat and Regroup

After retreating, the British regrouped and formed a new, strongly entrenched position on the north side of the Chippawa River. The victorious Americans halted. The two sides lost a combined total of about 750 men.

On 19 July, 1814, an American force burned St. Davids, Ontario. The main body of American troops under Brown moved out to march across the peninsula to isolate and defeat the remainder of Lieutenant General Drummond's corps. This strategy, if successful, would have left Burlington Heights and Upper Canada open and at the mercy of American forces, which already controlled Fort Erie and Queenston. However, fate took a decisive hand when Brown's forces accidentally encountered Drummond's advance guard, commanded by Lieutenant Colonel Thomas. It was 25 July, 1814, and the Battle of Lundy's Lane—the second bloodiest battle of the war—was set to begin.

THE NIAGARA FRONTIER

The Battle of Lundy's Lane

Drummond ordered a defensive line to be formed at the crest of the hill which commanded a full view of the surrounding countryside. At about 6 p.m. Brown's forces successfully advanced against the British left flank before being driven back themselves. When darkness descended, confusion was experienced by both armies. The Americans succeeded in repulsing the British from the hilltop and captured their guns. Riall, one of the British commanders, was wounded and captured. The American, Winfield Scott, was also wounded, along with three other American commanders.

Daylight and calm eventually returned. The battle was over. The loss of human life—staggering. Of the 3,200 British and American men who fought at Lundy's Lane, 1,738—more than 50 percent—were either killed or wounded.

Who won The Battle of Lundy's Lane? Canadian and British sources will usually say that the British were victorious, while American sources will give the battle to the Americans. That the results are clouded and disputed are not so much because of political bias, but because of the possible interpretations one can have about this confusing battle. The Americans certainly gained control of the crest and, in this author's view, can rightly claim victory. However, during a lull after the battle, the Americans regrouped away from the battlefield only to return to find the British firmly entrenched back on the hill. There was neither heart nor energy for more fighting and the Americans simply turned and retreated to Fort Erie. Lundy's Lane can perhaps best be said to be an

THE NIAGARA FRONTIER

American victory eventually won by the British.

After Lundy's Lane the British marched to Fort Erie, and on 15 August, 1814, they attacked the Americans. However, with their control of Lake Erie, secure supply lines, and effective advance guards who constantly harassed the British, the Americans broke the British siege. On 15 September, the Americans successfully fought their way out from Fort Erie, chasing the British to Chippawa. There remained one final heavy skirmish near Chippawa when the Americans were beaten back.

By 5 November evacuation of the Americans troops from Chippawa to Buffalo was completed before the arrival of winter. Before leaving, Brown gave orders for Fort Erie to be blown up.

The war formally came to a close on 24 December, 1814, with the signing of The Treaty of Ghent, although The Battle of New Orleans remained to be fought two weeks *after* the war officially ended with huge losses of British life. All conquests were to be returned—including Fort Niagara to the Americans. The borders were intact, unchanged since the war began. One might well ask: did this war accomplish anything?

The War of 1812 was clearly a mistake, but it served as a catalyst for nationalism on both sides of the border. Still a young nation, the United States became stronger, more unified and cohesive. It would go on to fight a bloody Civil War and still survive intact. Another nation, Canada, was about to be born. Its growing pains and the lessons it had learned gave impetus to confederation. Thus,

THE NIAGARA FRONTIER

Rhetoric from the War of 1812

"...we will teach the enemy this lesson: that a country defended by free men, enthusiastically devoted to the cause of their King and constitution, can never be conquered."

—*General Isaac Brock, July, 1812*—

"The annexation of Canada this year...will be a mere matter of marching, and will give us experience for the attack on Halifax the next, and the final expulsion of England from the American continent."

—*Thomas Jefferson, August, 1812*—

*There was a bold commander, brave General Brock by name,
Took shipping at Niagara and down to York he came,
He says "My gallant heroes, if you'll come along with me,
We'll fight those proud Yankees in the west of Canaday!"*

—*Anonymous, popular song from the War of 1812*—

THE NIAGARA FRONTIER

it can be said, that two of the most civilized nations on earth gained courage and determination and learned valuable lessons about themselves on the Niagara Frontier.

But there was also a victim nation—that of the Indian...which lost all there was to lose.

"Lo, the poor Indian! whose untutor'd mind
Sees God in clouds, or hears him in the wind:
His soul proud Science never taught to stray
Far as the solar walk or milky way:
Yet simple nature to his hope has giv'n,
Behind the cloud-topp'd hill, an humbler heav'n.

—Alexander Pope,
An Essay on Man, 1688-1744—

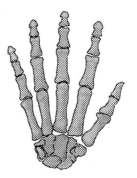

THE NIAGARA FRONTIER

Chapter 5
The Republic of Navy Island

*"The nations are fallen, and thou still art young,
The sun is but rising when others have set;
And though Slavery's cloud o'er thy morning hath hung,
The fall tide of Freedom shall beam round thee yet."*

—Extract from William Lyon Mackenzie's appeal to arms in a handbill entitled "Independence" dated Friday, 1 December 1837, at Toronto—

To commit high treason is to betray one's government or the sovereign head of one's nation. At any time it is a very serious crime. During the War of 1812, in Upper Canada, high treason was regarded by the British as being very worst of crimes and those convicted of it were subjected to the harshest of penalties.

THE NIAGARA FRONTIER

The Ancaster Bloody Assize

In Ancaster, just south of Hamilton, men were on trial for treason during May and June of 1814. All were followers of Abraham Marcle, a community leader in Ancaster, who had lived in the United States until his arrival in Canada in about 1805.

During a raid by a Loyalist militia, near Chatham (Ontario), two rebels were killed, 40 others were captured, while Marcle and one other man escaped. About 15 of those arrested were Canadian settlers who were first jailed in York and then taken to Ancaster. In Ancaster, the trial of the 19 who were accused of treason began on 23 May, 1814. Of those 19 men, 14 were convicted, one pleaded guilty, and four were acquitted. Those convicted in what became known as the Ancaster Bloody Assize, received the following, established, though still grisly, sentence:

"You are each of you to be taken to the place from which you came, and from thence you are to be drawn on hurdles to the place of execution where you must be hanged by the neck, but not until you are dead, for you must be cut down while you are alive, and your entrails taken out and burned before your faces, then your head must be cut off and your bodies divided into four quarters, and your heads and quarters to be at the King's disposal. And may God have mercy on your souls."

The condemned men received permission to apply for clemency; six were saved from the gallows, and eight met their maker on 20 July, 1814, at what is now the Hamilton Cemetery on York Boulevard. An account of the hangings was given to a newspaper

THE NIAGARA FRONTIER

reporter by an observer, John Ryckman, in an article that appeared in **The Hamilton Spectator** on 4 October 1880.

"Later, the narrator (John Ryckman) saw eight men hanged the other side of Locke Street, near Dundurn. It was during the war, and these men were accused of having furnished provisions to the enemy. A rude gallows was prepared with eight nooses, and the victims were placed in two wagons, four in each, and drawn under the gallows. They stood upon boards laid across the wagon, and after the nooses had been adjusted the wagons were drawn away and the unfortunate traitors were left to strangle to death. The contortions of the poor men so shook the loosely constructed gallows that a heavy brace became loosened and fell, striking one of the victims on the head and killing him instantly, thus relieving him from the torture of the rope. After the men had been duly strangled their heads were chopped off and exhibited as the heads of traitors. Seven of the victims seemed willing to die, but the eighth pleaded for his life and said that what he had done was simply out of a feeling of hospitality, and that he did not know whom he was entertaining. The execution was conducted by Sheriff Merritt, of Niagara."

Divided loyalties and discontent with those who ruled Upper Canada did not die with the end of the War of 1812 or with the executions of traitors. In 1819, a prominent landowner, Robert Fleming Gourlay, was put on trial at Newark for publicly speaking out (sedition) against Upper Canada's ruling authority known as The Family Compact, and was duly banished from Upper Canada.

THE NIAGARA FRONTIER

Unrest and Conflict Continue

The Frontier experienced vigorous economic development during the 1820s with the building of the Erie Canal in 1825, to connect New York City and Buffalo, while on the west side the Welland Canal was built in 1829, to allow shipping to pass between Lakes Ontario and Erie. Thus, the Niagara Frontier remained a vital and strategic location both for Britain and the United States.

Much of the rest of Upper Canada and, in particular, Lower Canada did not share this economic vigor. In the 1830s food shortages worsened the tensions that already existed between French Canadian habitants and the British minority ruling class, and this ultimately led to violence. This unrest spilled over into Upper Canada where there was considerable opposition towards those who ruled. Those in power (The Family Compact), were much criticized for government patronage, and for favoritism towards the Church of England, its followers, and recent English immigrants.

Much of the popular opposition towards this oligarchic form of government came from so-called Late Loyalists who arrived in Canada from the United States just prior to the War of 1812.

William Lyon Mackenzie

The Niagara Frontier did not experience the same degree of unrest and conflict that was to occur in York and the rest of Upper and Lower Canada until near the end of the uprisings. However, in

THE NIAGARA FRONTIER

1837, one of the leaders of the rebellion in Upper Canada, William Lyon Mackenzie, organized a provisional government of Upper Canada with its headquarters based on Navy Island, in the Niagara River.

William Lyon Mackenzie, born in Dundee, Scotland in 1795, was a journalist who wrote with a strong sense of social justice. Mackenzie was Toronto's first mayor and a member of the House of Assembly for York County. He was also the leading critic of Upper Canada's ruling oligarchic elite. Continually reelected into office until his defeat in 1836, Mackenzie began to organize armed resistance against the ruling government in Upper Canada, but fled Toronto for the Niagara Frontier, in December, 1837, after what might be kindly described as an attempted coup d'état. Escaping via the Niagara Peninsula, he reached Buffalo where he began to organize his new provisional government. Bonds were sold to fund the new government, and weapons and money were obtained from American sympathizers and supporters. In addition, an American steam vessel called the **Caroline** was made available to transport supplies from the mainland to Navy Island. By 13 December, 1837, Mackenzie declared Navy Island to be the headquarters of his new provisional government. Two Americans, Thomas Jefferson Sutherland and Rensselaer Van Rensselaer, were to coordinate military activities, along with 300 - 400 followers, most of whom were unemployed Americans.

The Navy Island Incident

Navy Island was Canadian territory as specified in the Treaty of Ghent and is, incidentally, the only Canadian island in the

THE NIAGARA FRONTIER

William Lyon Mackenzie
Courtesy: Ontario Archives, reference ACC 2242 S3874

THE NIAGARA FRONTIER

The Burning of the Caroline
Courtesy: The Buffalo and Erie County Historical Society
#21549-1

THE NIAGARA FRONTIER

Niagara River. The government of Upper Canada grew alarmed at the rebels' strong position and so dispatched Colonel Allan Napier MacNab and his militia to deal with them. Bombardment of the island had little effect, so MacNab ordered Lieutenant Andrew Drew, a veteran of the Royal Navy, to destroy the rebel's ship, **Caroline**, it being their only means of transportation and communication with the mainland. The **Caroline** was docked at Schlosser, New York, which was indisputably American territory. On 29 December, 1837, during a night raid, the Canadian force invaded Schlosser (and, therefore, the United States), and set fire to the **Caroline**. One American, Amos Durfee, was killed during the attack. The blazing **Caroline** was set adrift and plunged to its complete destruction over Niagara Falls.

The Navy Island incident very nearly reignited the War of 1812. Fortunately, tensions eased when Britain agreed to pay the United States for her losses, and the Americans agreed to acquit a militia-man named Alexander McLeod, who was on trial for murdering the American during the attack on the **Caroline**. Both MacNab and Drew were honoured in Upper Canada and MacNab also received a knighthood. Mackenzie was later arrested in Buffalo by U.S. officials for breach of the Neutrality Act. Rensselaer Van Rensselaer was placed under arrest after ordering the evacuation of Navy Island on 14 January 1838, while Thomas Jefferson Sutherland continued to fight along the border with various American patriot military groups.

A Short-lived Invasion

There was one more attempt at invasion. On 11 June, 1838, 26

THE NIAGARA FRONTIER

Grand Island / Navy Island

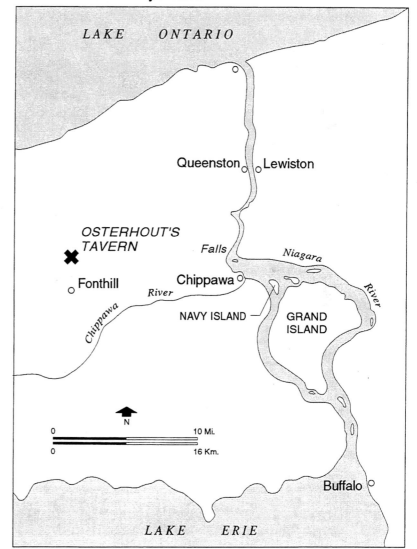

THE NIAGARA FRONTIER

men sympathetic to Mackenzie's cause, and under the leadership of James Morrow (some sources state Moreau), crossed the Niagara River from Grand Island and made their way to the Short Hills, just north of present-day Fonthill, Ontario. There they were soon joined by 22 others and together attacked a party of 13 Queen's Lancers who were stationed at Osterhout's Tavern, at the then thriving village of St. John's, about 3.5 km (2.3 miles) north of Fonthill, Ontario. The rebels gradually succeeded in forcing their way onto the first floor of the building with the Lancers cornered on the second floor. Threatened with death by fire, the Lancers surrendered to the invaders. Their success was short-lived, however, as another detachment of Lancers soon arrived and completely overwhelmed the invaders with 31 of their number captured and the rest dispersed. Punishment was swift and severe. Some of the invaders were sentenced to death, with the rest being banished to Tasmania (an island off the south coast of Australia). In the end, though, only Morrow was actually hanged.

The rebellion in Upper Canada was essentially over except for one final act. On Good Friday, 17 April 1840, Benjamin Lott (some sources say Lett) and a group of rebels crossed the Niagara River at Queenston, scaled its heights, and placed gunpowder at the monument dedicated to General Brock. The blast irreparably damaged the monument, but it remained standing until 1853 when work on the present impressive structure began. Costing $50,000 and paid for by private donations, it was completed in 1856. The Brock Monument of today stands 56 metres high (184 feet), about 15 metres (49 feet) higher than its predecessor. Inside are 235 steps that will take observers to the top.

THE NIAGARA FRONTIER

Although the Frontier's strategic importance now began to fade, it would remain an important threshold through the 1840s, 50s and 60s for those who were to pass through it on their way from slavery to freedom via the Underground Railroad.

"A little rebellion now and then is a good thing."

—Thomas Jefferson, 1743-1826—

THE NIAGARA FRONTIER

THE NIAGARA FRONTIER

Chapter 6
Rail Trail to Freedom

**"TO BE SOLD
A STRONG NEGRO WOMAN
about 30 years of age. Understands cookery,
laundry, and the taking care of poultry.
N.B. She can also dress ladies' hair.
ENQUIRE OF THE PRINTERS"**

—Advertisement, Upper Canada Gazette, December 1800—

In 1793, in Upper Canada, slavery as an institution began to weaken, as legislation introduced by Governor John Graves Simcoe challenged its legal status. Slavery ended, both legally and practically, in 1834, when it was abolished throughout the entire British Empire.

THE NIAGARA FRONTIER

William Lyon Mackenzie, whose writings and vitriol directed towards the ruling elite of Upper Canada sparked much of the rebellion there in 1837, had also written passionately against other forms of social injustice, especially slavery. The following is an extract from his paper, ***The Colonial Advocate***, circa 1832:

"One day last summer a poor black girl, who had escaped from the whip-lash to this side of the water, was seized on a Sunday near Queenston in broad daylight, between eleven and noon, by two hired scoundrels who hauled and pulled her through that village, she screaming and crying in the most piteous and heartrending manner and her ruffian cream-coloured tormentors laughing at her distress and amusing the villagers with the cock-and-bull story that she had stolen five hundred dollars."

Another notable incident occurred around 1837, in what is now Niagara-on-the-Lake, Ontario, when a slave named Solomon Moseby (some sources state Mosely) escaped from his owner in Louisville, Kentucky. While British law permitted former slaves to remain in Canada, this case was complicated by the fact that Moseby had indeed committed a crime by stealing a horse. On those grounds the authorities held him in jail to await extradition to the United States. A crowd of some 200 to 400 blacks assembled at the jail, under the leadership of Herbert Holmes, a local preacher and teacher, to try to prevent the extradition of Moseby, who would most certainly be returned to his master and killed both as a punishment and a warning to other slaves.

In due course the sheriff brought Moseby out of the jail under

THE NIAGARA FRONTIER

The Underground Railroad

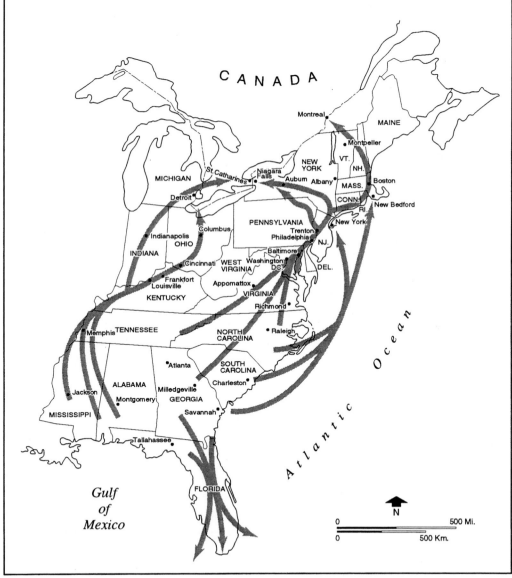

Source: Kathy King, Niagara Gazette.

THE NIAGARA FRONTIER

armed escort to a wagon which was to transport him to an awaiting ferry. Herbert Holmes and another man, Jacob Green, grabbed the reins of the horses. In an instant Holmes was shot dead and Green was bayoneted to death. An athletic Moseby, however, made good his escape, eventually travelling to England, and returning later to the Niagara area where he was reportedly reunited with his wife. Though technically interfering with the due process of law, Holmes and Green were generally regarded as martyrs for the greater cause by allowing another man to remain free.

The Underground Railroad

In the United States opposition towards slavery grew in the northern states, resulting in the passing of The Fugitive Slave Act of 1850. This act, though well-intentioned, proved to be compromise legislation. Though it barred slavery in the north and in future states to the west, it still permitted slave owners to recapture former slaves living in the north. It was during this time, in the 1840s, 50s and 60s that the Underground Railroad operated at its peak.

The Underground Railroad was an informal series of safe houses located strategically throughout the United States and Canada where runaway slaves were housed and given assistance by anti-slavery men and women, many of whom were Quakers, Coventers, Methodists, or of other deeply held religious affiliations. It consisted of 'stations' that were the safe houses, and 'station-masters' who were the proprietors of safe houses. Those who aided the fugitive slaves were 'conductors', while the 'passengers' or 'freight' were the slaves themselves.

THE NIAGARA FRONTIER

The Journey North to Freedom

Most of the slaves who passed through the Niagara Frontier came by way of Ohio, Pennsylvania, or New York City, after a six to eight week journey from the south. Another five major routes leading to Canada, Mexico and the Caribbean, plus many other secondary routes, comprised this invisible network.

The Underground Railroad got its name from a story about a Kentucky plantation owner who was closing in on the trail of an escaped slave in Ohio. When all trace of the slave suddenly vanished, he said, *"He must have gone down an underground road"*. Through usage *"Underground Road"* eventually evolved into *"Underground Railroad"* because of the growing prominence of the railways in the mid 1800s.

A slave family in the south, intent upon escape to freedom, began by storing food, and by making knapsacks or carriers to carry both food and any young children. The father would then have contaced the one slave on the plantation who knew of outside contacts. Escape usually took place on a Saturday night, as Sunday festivities meant that the escaping slaves would not generally be missed until Monday morning. The family travelled on foot only at night, covering no more than 30 kilometers (18 miles) until the first safe house was reached. There food and shelter and directions to the next safe house were provided. The family was instructed to trust only other blacks or people dressed like Quakers or Amish.

THE NIAGARA FRONTIER

The first major destination was Philadelphia with its very active anti-slavery movement. From Philadelphia the family proceeded to Elmira, New York, crossing the Catskill Mountains. From Elmira it journeyed to Corning, Dansville, Covington, Warsaw, and eventually to Batavia, New York. From there it headed west through Pembrook, Clarence, or Bowmanville, and on to Buffalo.

After being hidden a few days in Buffalo, at the Michigan Avenue Baptist Church, the last day of the perilous journey arrived. A ferry crew would usher the family aboard its craft, destined for Fort Erie, across the river, with all possible secrecy. While New York was then a free-state, slave owners still legally and actively pursued runaway slaves there, so secrecy and evasion were essential. Once the ferry docked at Fort Erie, the family would wait for the other passengers to disembark, then furtively make its way to a large red brick building with white pillars in front of it. This was Bertie Hall, standing at the intersection of Niagara Boulevard and Phipps Street. Many other fleeing slaves crossed the Niagara River by means of the railway bridges that were in existence at that time.

After their arrival in Fort Erie, the family would stay another few days at Bertie Hall until work and accommodation for them could be found. There were jobs to be had locally, cutting wood for the ferries and railways, and over the years black communities took root in Fort Erie and St. Catharines. Josiah Henson and Harriet Tubman were two of the Frontier's most prominent black leaders of the time. Former slaves themselves, they helped many others to freedom. The town of Dresden, east of Windsor,

THE NIAGARA FRONTIER

Ontario, was founded by Henson and his followers to serve as a black community. Henson, who lived in Fort Erie for four years, was the model, it is said, for Uncle Tom in Harriet Beecher Stowe's anti-slavery novel, *Uncle Tom's Cabin*, while Tubman was known as the 'Moses' of her people.

The Birth of a Movement

After about 1880, Fort Erie's black population dispersed when jobs relying on the cutting of hardwood began to disappear. However, Fort Erie continued to play an important part in black history when, in 1905, it hosted a meeting of the Niagara Movement at the Erie Beach Hotel, after this embryonic black activist group was denied accommodation in Buffalo. Freedom of speech, freedom of the press, the right to vote, and universal education were the Niagara Movement's tenets, and it provided the organizational framework for the future N.A.A.C.P. (National Association for the Advancement of Colored People).

Despite former political differences that had often led to ill will and war, both nations bordering the Niagara Frontier were beginning to share common visions of responsible democracy and basic personal freedoms. But there was still a rocky road ahead.

Tensions during the Civil War had been great along the Niagara Frontier, but the confict had not directly affected Canada. After the Civil War ended the Frontier was to be used as springboard for yet another invasion, not by armies of blue as was originally feared, but by armies of green clad men. These invaders were

THE NIAGARA FRONTIER

Fenians from the northern United States, who were allied with the Fenian group in Ireland.

"O Master and Mistress, don't come after me
For I cannot be your slave any more
I'm under British laws, I'm beneath the lion's paws
And he'll growl if you come near the shore."

—Anonymous—

THE NIAGARA FRONTIER

Chapter 7
The Fenians Are Coming!

"We are the Fenian Brotherhood, skilled in the arts of war,
And we're going to fight for Ireland, and the land that we adore.
Many battles we have won, along with the boys in blue,
And we'll go and capture Canada, for we've nothing else to do!"

—Extract from a Fenian poster, Jackdaw, No. C21—

Fenian is another term for Irish Republican Brotherhood, an extremist Irish political movement, founded in the United States after the Civil War. Its intention was to secure Irish independence from Britain through violent means. The Brotherhood grew simultaneously in Ireland and the U.S., with the U.S. wing becoming a very prominent force with thousands of armed, unemployed northern veterans of Irish descent. The movement consisted of two wings: one advocated direct rebellion against Britain in Ireland, while the other advocat-

THE NIAGARA FRONTIER

ed attacking Britain indirectly, through Canada, its North American colony.

After the Civil War, tension was high in what was then Canada West and Canada East. Britain had supported the South both materially and spiritually during the war, and this fueled American antipathy for anything British. New York papers predicted Union armies would someday march victoriously through Canada, and the U.S. government under Andrew Johnson never censured Fenian leaders after they had approached the U.S. government for its policy towards a Canada under Fenian control.

Canadian fears of invasion by blue armies from the North eventually proved groundless, but fears of invasion by green armies proved correct. While an anticipated invasion of 17 March, 1866 (St. Patrick's Day) did not materialize, in April the Fenians did strike suddenly in the east at an island off the coast of New Brunswick, forcing the lone customs officer on duty at the time to surrender. The U.S. government took action after this incident by detaining and confiscating shipments of Fenian arms, and this did result in the eventual dispersal of the Fenians on the east coast.

To offset this setback, Colonel John O'Neill of the Fenian army planned a new offensive. By striking at Canada West, he could secure a base of operations on the Niagara Peninsula for a larger Fenian force to follow.

O'Neill was an experienced cavalry man. Born in Ireland, in

THE NIAGARA FRONTIER

1834, he emigrated to the United States, where he served with the Northern Army. There he gained the reputation of being a tough, brave, smart, decisive and resourceful military commander. By 31 May, 1866, he had arrived in Buffalo as the head of a Fenian force of about 1,000 men, consisting of four regiments and one independent company. After training there for a brief period, O'Neill ordered the Fenian force to march to Black Rock, a Buffalo suburb, where it embarked for Canada in the early hours of 1 June, 1866.

Invasion!

On the Canadian side, on 31 May, 1866, a British consul in Buffalo had warned authorities of the very strong possibility of an attack by the Fenians. A wired message was sent the following day confirming that the Fenians had in fact invaded Canada at Fort Erie. Canadian militiamen were dispatched to both Port Colborne, under Lieutenant Colonel Booker, and to St. Catharines, under Colonel Peacocke. Their task was to secure the Welland Canal, and to contain and check the Fenian advance. Colonel Peacocke, a British army regular, was given overall command of the Canadian force of about 800 men.

Peacocke's forces were to advance towards Chippawa to link up with Booker in the vicinity of Ridgeway in preparation for a concentrated attack upon the Fenians. While Booker executed his orders without delay by marching east to Ridgeway, Peacocke inexplicably departed two hours late from his camp at St. Catharines and took a circuitous route via the River Road. This

THE NIAGARA FRONTIER

resulted in a critical delay of four to five hours in the arrival of his forces at Ridgeway.

Another Canadian force of 100 men under Lieutenant Colonel Dennis sailed to Fort Erie in a large tug called the **W.T. Robb**. Dennis's original orders were to obtain some large cannon for a steamer that had been ordered by Colonel Peacocke, and then use the steamer to patrol the Niagara River. When both the steamer and the cannon proved to be unavailable, Dennis obtained the **W.T. Robb** and set sail in it without first awaiting Peacocke's new orders necessitated by the unavailability of the large guns.

The Battle of Ridgeway

When O'Neill's scouts advised him of Booker's advance, the Fenian commander took advantage of some high ground along Ridge Road at Ridgeway and met the Canadian force at 8 a.m. on 2 June, 1866.

The debacle that followed was all over by 10 a.m. During the battle a Canadian, either an officer or a soldier, had mistakingly cried *"Cavalry"* causing the Canadian force to form a 'Square for Cavalry'. Booker attempted to regroup his charges when it became evident that the warning was a mistake, but fierce Fenian firepower easily decimated the easy target that the tight square presented to them. What was left of the Canadian force retreated to Port Colborne.

THE NIAGARA FRONTIER

The Battle of Fort Erie

Meanwhile, Lieutenant Colonel Dennis was enjoying some success against small bands of Fenian raiders as he sailed along Lake Erie's shoreline towards Fort Erie. Arriving at Fort Erie, Dennis decided to leave a small force in charge of Fenian prisoners. However, news of the imminent arrival of the main Fenian force changed his mind. During the late afternoon of 2 June, the main Fenian army met and quickly defeated the Canadian force which had positioned itself with its back to the water and was thus trapped.

The towns of Fort Erie and Ridgeway had been largely deserted by the time the fighting began. Fort Erie's reeve, Dr. Peter T. Kempson, had the distinction of being the town's only official to surrender to an invading army. The Fenians generally treated the general population well with very little damage or loss of property other than some horses that were reported stolen. The total amount of compensation later claimed by the population was just under $6,000. Considering that it was an invading army, the Fenians left a good impression upon the general population with their disciplined and respectful behavior. During the Battle of Fort Erie, crowds had formed on the Buffalo side, cheering the Fenians on, and debating the strengths and weaknesses of each manoeuvre as if the spectacle were a game of football.

This Fenian venture, despite its military success, was doomed to failure. President Andrew Johnson, the 17th President of the United States, issued a proclamation banning any further Fenian

THE NIAGARA FRONTIER

Battles of Ridgeway and Fort Erie, 2 June, 1866

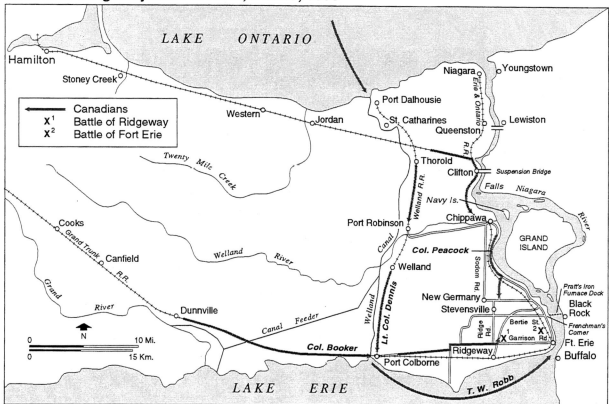

Source: Senior, Hereward, The Last Invasion of Canada, Dundurn Press Toronto, 1991.

THE NIAGARA FRONTIER

incursions into Canada. Colonel O'Neill, upon learning that Fenian men and arms had been intercepted by U.S. forces at Buffalo, realized that the Fenian position was untenable and withdrew to the United States where his forces were intercepted by the warship **U.S.S. Michigan** and arrested for breach of the Neutrality Laws.

Thus, the Fenian threat faded along the Niagara Frontier although Fenians continued to cause problems in Canada. Fenians existed until 1916 but caused no more difficulty for Canada after 1871. They staged two further unsuccessful Canadian raids: one into Quebec in 1870, and another into Manitoba, in 1871, led by O'Neill. The latter was dispersed by U.S. authorities. (It is interesting to note here that Louis Riel, the Métis leader who would later be branded as a traitor and hanged by the Canadian Government, had earlier offered the government his assistance in raising a Métis force to resist any Fenian attack directed at Manitoba.) In Britain the Fenians were held responsible for deaths resulting from violence in both London and Manchester.

The Fenian Legacy

The fact that the Battles of Ridgeway and Fort Erie, 2 June, 1866, were so closely followed by Canadian Confederation on 1 July, 1867, is no coincidence. While Confederation undoubtedly would have occurred in any event, the Fenian attacks undoubtedly accelerated the birth of the new nation of Canada. The leaders of four separate provinces were now clearly able to see how vul-

THE NIAGARA FRONTIER

nerable they were in their disunity, and how they could no longer depend on Britain to provide for their defense.

"What experience and history teach us,
however, is this, that peoples and governments
have never learned anything from history."

—Georg Hegel, 1837—

THE NIAGARA FRONTIER

Epilogue

On 5 June 1866, Fenian riflemen at Youngstown, New York, spent much of their day taking potshots at what is now the town of Niagara-on-the-Lake, Ontario, and later dispersed. After this last military action, the Niagara Frontier began to assume its present peaceful reputation as part of the world's longest undefended border.

Touring the Niagara Frontier Today

For a sense of the history of the Niagara Frontier, the following route might be considered. Many of the locations along it are not generally as well-known as landmarks such as Brock's Monument and Forts Erie and Niagara but are, nonetheless, of historical significance. But then, throughout the Niagara Frontier, history is so much a part of the fabric that it touches virtually everything.

THE NIAGARA FRONTIER

South of the Falls

The following route follows the Niagara Parkway in a northerly direction along the Canadian side of the river.

At Fort Erie, one can still see Bertie Hall at the corners of Phipps Street and Niagara Boulevard. A red building with the white pillars, Bertie Hall was once a safe house for fugitive slaves and an important part of the Underground Railroad.

Heading north along the Niagara Parkway the Niagara Recreation Trail begins at the outskirts of Fort Erie. This paved trail follows the course of the Niagara River with very few interruptions and ends at Niagara-on-the-Lake. Walkers, runners, cyclists and in-line skaters abound during the better weather.

Further along the Parkway is the marina that was once the site of Miller's Bay Shipyard. Many freed blacks were able to find work there. At Black Creek, there is a building dated 1828 that at various times served as a safe house, a coach stop, a jail, a hotel, a post office and a restaurant, and was visited by Grover Cleveland, the 22nd and 24th president of the United States.

Nearing the outskirts of Niagara Falls, an old metal scow (barge) remains hung up on the rocks a few hundred metres above the Horseshoe Falls. This relic recalls an extraordinary event from 7 August, 1918, when it broke loose from a tug during dredging operations in the upper part of the river. Two men were on board as it plowed through the upper rapids on its way to destruction. James

THE NIAGARA FRONTIER

Bertie Hall, Fort Erie, Ontario
Photo by the author

THE NIAGARA FRONTIER

Harris, age 53, of Buffalo, and Gustav Lofberg, age 51, a Swedish sailor, though badly frightened, both reacted smartly by opening up the scow's bottom hatches. This allowed the scow to ground itself upon a ledge, near the edge of the cataract, where it remains to this day. Rescue crews on shore, some 250 metres (750 feet) away, shot ropes to the scow. A rescue basket was attached to the ropes but the lines became entangled. Red Hill, a well-known local daredevil and discharged soldier, came upon the scene and offered his help. Gassed by his own army and given six months to live by doctors, Hill had been sent home from the World War raging in Europe. A rescue basket carried Hill to the halfway point, whereupon he climbed out and proceeded to pull himself along the main rope, hand over hand, until he reached the point where he could free the tangled lines. One by one, all three men returned safely to shore in the basket. Incidentally, Hill proved the army doctors wrong and lived for another 24 years! The scow has been said to be deteriorating for years now and a piece of Niagara history is likely to disappear someday.

North of the Falls

Leaving the Falls behind and following the winding Parkway along the top of the Niagara Gorge, the Canadian and American Hydro Plants dominate the skyline. Shortly Brock's Monument at Queenston Heights comes into view. There is much history at this site, but one little known fact is that the children's wading pool there is built upon the foundations of what was Fort Drummond! (Fort Drummond had been built by the British to protect the northern end of Portage Road). Also at Queenston is the Church

THE NIAGARA FRONTIER

of St. Saviour, built at the river's edge under the most idyllic circumstances. It commemorates Sir Isaac Brock.

Birthplace of the Falls

The birthplace of the Falls can be viewed from the roadside viewing area halfway down the hill leading to the town of Queenston. Walk back up the hill a short way to wooden stairs that lead to the Redan Battery site. From this location can be seen the Eldridge Terrace, an outcrop of layers of rock lying some 11 meters (35 feet) below and to the right of a large mansion like house situated on the top of the escarpment on the American side. This is where waters from ancient Lake Tonawanda first began to spill over into ancestral Lake Ontario to form the Falls. From this point, the Falls retreated 11 kilometres (7 miles) upstream to their present location. Incidentally, the trails that parallel the river at the bottom are actually old railway beds.

Heading out of Queenston towards Niagara-on-the-Lake, a miniature wayside chapel offers spiritual relief. Despite the large numbers of tourists who flock to Niagara-on-the-Lake in the summer months, the town is not to be missed. Some of the homes and churches the visitor will see there date from the end of the War of 1812. Buildings from this period can also be found in Youngstown, New York and Lewiston, New York.

Standing by the riverside at Niagara-on-the-Lake early on a quiet Sunday morning, before the crowds and the hum of motor traffic arrive to break the spell, it is very easy to imagine the scene as it

THE NIAGARA FRONTIER

The Redan Gun Battery Site, Queenston, Ontario
Photo by the author

THE NIAGARA FRONTIER

Stained Glass Window, Brock Memorial Church of St. Saviour, Queenston, Ontario
Photo by the author

This stained glass is dedicated to the memory of Major General Sir Isaac Brock. The Brock family crest is depicted at the top of the window. Below the cannon on the right is the coat of arms of the Dominion of Canada when it consisted of only four provinces—Ontario, Quebec, New Brunswick and Nova Scotia. Various military hardware are leaning against the cannon to the left and right of the central figures of Joshua and Archangel, Michael. This window faces west and its principal colours are shades of green, gold, blue and scarlet. The window was made by Mr. Joseph McCausland of Toronto in 1881.

THE NIAGARA FRONTIER

might have been two centuries before: weatherbeaten men unfurling the sails of schooners, while others unload from the holds barrels of pork bound for the garrison at Fort Niagara. Indians of the region, pulling ashore their canoes piled high with furs and eagerly anticipating the bartering and trading that will have to be done that day.

We cannot relive the past, but through the conscientious conservation of our natural and historical sites, we can at least preserve enough of the past to give future generations some sense of how it was back then!

THE NIAGARA FRONTIER

Appendix 1
OVER THE FALLS

A selected list of those who made the plunge,
some deliberately and some by accident

24 Oct 1901: **Annie Taylor** in a wooden barrel—survived.
25 July 1911: **Bobby Leach** in a steel drum—survived.
11 July 1920: **Charles Stephens** in a wooden barrel—died.
4 July 1928: **Jean Lussier** in a rubber ball—survived.
4 July 1930: **George Stathakis** in inner tubes—died.
5 Aug 1951: **William Red Hill Jr** in inner tubes—died
9 July 1960: **Roger Woodward** in a lifejacket—survived
15 July 1961: **Nathan Boya** in a rubber ball—survived.
3 July 1984: **Karel Soucek** in a metal barrel—survived..
19 Aug 1985: **Steven Trotter** in a metal barrel—survived.
5 Oct 1985: **Dave Munday** in a metal barrel—survived.
6 June 1990: **Jesse Sharp** in a kayak—died.
1 Oct 1995: **Robert Overacker**, water bike with parachute—died.

(in the period Jan-Sept 1996, at least 5 persons are known to have been
swept over the Falls)

THE NIAGARA FRONTIER

While daredevil stunts are now illegal and strictly forbidden, they still occur from time to time. As do unforeseen accidents.

An Unfortunate Spectacle

On 8 September, 1827, the schooner **Michigan** with a load of animals plunged over the Falls in a disgusting spectacle sponsored by local merchants. The boat had in it a buffalo, one or two bears, a goose, an eagle tied to the ship and other animals. The buffalo and several other animals were thrown overboard and perished, while the **Michigan** rocked its way through the upper rapids and over the Falls to its complete destruction. The bear(s) jumped ship and made it safely to an island. Of those animals who actually went over the Falls, only the goose survived.

THE NIAGARA FRONTIER

Appendix 2
FALLS' PERSONALITIES
Just a few of the many famous visitors to Niagara

James Monroe (U.S. President), 1817
Charles Dickens, 1841
Jenny Lind (Swedish singer), 1850 & 51.
Abraham Lincoln, 1857
George Armstrong Custer, 1869
Queen Victoria, 1877
Oscar Wilde, 1882
Pëtr Ilyich Tchaikovsky, 1891
Theodore Roosevelt, 1899
Madame Curie, 1921
Dick Powell, 1939
Shirley Temple, 1944
Andrie Gromyko, 1946
Gene Autry, 1950
Marilyn Monroe, 1953

THE NIAGARA FRONTIER

Rudy Vallee, 1960
President J.F. Kennedy, 1960
Richard Nixon, 1960
Archbishop of Canterbury, 1960
Jack Benny, 1966
Moshe Dayan, 1974
Roger Bannister (British Olympic runner), 1977
Christopher Reeve, 1979
Margot Kidder, 1979
Hosni Mubarak, 1983
Li Xiannian (Chinese President), 1985
Jean Beliveau (Canadian ice-hockey star), 1992
&
many, many others.

Sir Winston Churchill also visited Niagara several times during his long life. When asked, after his second visit, whether the Falls looked the same as when he first saw them, Churchill thought for a moment, then replied: *"Well, the principle seems the same. The water still keeps falling over."*

Niagara Falls, the 'Honeymoon Capital of the World', has often provided the setting for films with romantic themes. Among the more famous are: *Niagara*, with Marilyn Monroe and Joseph Cotten, and *Superman II*, with Christopher Reeve and Margot Kidder.

THE NIAGARA FRONTIER

Appendix 3

FACTS AND FIGURES

Length of Niagara River—55 kilometres (33 miles)
First bridge across Niagara Gorge—1848
Peace Bridge, date of opening—1927
Rainbow Bridge, date of opening—1941
Population of Niagara Falls, Ontario (1904)—est. 7,000
Population of Niagara Falls, Ontario (1986)—72,107
Arrival of railway in Niagara Falls, Ontario—1853
Total annual visitors to Niagara Falls—est. 12—14 million
Height of American Falls—64 metres (208 feet)
Width of American Falls—305 metres (991 feet)
Height of Horseshoe Falls—54 metres (176 feet)
Width of Horseshoe Falls—675 metres (2,194 feet)
Niagara Falls, total average flow—170 million litres per minute

THE NIAGARA FRONTIER

Acknowledgements

The author would like to thank the following institutions, their representatives, and other individuals for their kind assistance and expert guidance received during the many months of research for this book:

- Hamilton Central Public Library
- Niagara Falls (Ontario) Public Library
- Buffalo and Erie County Historical Society
- McMaster University
- Jane Davies, Fort Erie Museum
- Buffalo & Erie County Public Library
- Niagara Falls (New York) Public Library
- Woodland Indian Cultural Educational Centre, Brantford, Ontario
- National Archives, Ottawa
- Archives of Ontario, Toronto
- Royal Ontario Museum, Toronto
- Battlefield House, Stoney Creek, Ontario

THE NIAGARA FRONTIER

- University of Michigan Museum of Anthropology
- Willoughby Township Museum
- Niagara-on-the-Lake Public Library
- Fort Erie Public Library
- Lundy's Lane Historical Society
- Ancaster Public Library
- Andrew Armitage, Owen Sound Public Library
- Town of Pelham Public Library
- Canon John Hesketh, St. Catharines, Ontario
- Kevin O'Halloran, Simcoe, Ontario
- Nan Doan, Niagara Falls, Ontario

The modern maps used throughout this book were drawn by Barry Levely in the Environmental Studies Cartographic Centre, University of Waterloo.

THE NIAGARA FRONTIER

Picture Credits

THE NIAGARA FRONTIER

THE NIAGARA FRONTIER

Selected Bibliography

Bassett, John/ **Petrie**, Roy. *Laura Secord*, Fitzhenry & Whiteside Limited, Toronto, 1974, 1981.

Berton, Pierre. *The Invasion of Canada, 1812 - 1813*, McClelland and Stewart, Toronto, 1980.

— *Flames Across the Border, 1813 - 1814*, McClelland and Stewart, Toronto, 1981.

Bevan, George. A. *The Role of the Niagara Frontier in Canadian Military History (A Study in Historical Geography)*; Thesis, McMaster University, Hamilton, 1948.

THE NIAGARA FRONTIER

Braider, Donald. *The Niagara*, Rinehart and Winston, New York, 1972.

Donaldson, Gordon. *Niagara! The Eternal Circus*, Doubleday, Toronto, 1979.

Ellis, Chris J./**Ferris**, Neal, Editors. *The Archaeology of Southern Ontario to A.D. 1650.* Occasional Publication of the London Chapter, OAS, Number 5, 1990.

Flint, David. *William Lyon Mackenzie: Rebel Against Authority*, Oxford University Press, Toronto, 1971.

Greenhill, Ralph/**Mahone**y, Thomas. *Niagara*, University of Toronto Press, Toronto, 1969.

Guillet, Edwin. *Early Life in Upper Canada*, Reprinted by University of Toronto Press, Toronto, 1963.

Harper, Russell. *The Early History of Haldimand County: The Grand River Sachem*, Harrison & Arrell Martindale, Publishers, 1950.

Hennepin, Louis. *A New Discovery of a Vast Country in America*, Reprinted by Coles Publishing Co., Toronto, 1974.

Hill, Norbert S. Jr.. *Words of Power: Voices of Indian America*, Fulcrum Publishing, Golden Co., 1994.

THE NIAGARA FRONTIER

Hitsman, Mackay. *The Incredible War of 1812: A Military History*, University of Toronto Press, Toronto and Buffalo, 1965.

Holley, George. *The Falls of Niagara*, A.C. Armstrong & Son, New York, 1883.

Jameson, Anna. *The Falls of Niagara, Being a Complete Guide to...the Great Cataract*, Nelson Co., London, 1858.

Johnston, C.M. *The Head of the Lake: A History of Wentworth County*, Published by Wentworth County Council, Hamilton, Revised 1967.

Kenyon, W. A. *The Grimsby Site: A Historic Neutral Cemetery*, Royal Ontario Museum, Toronto, 1992.

McKinsey, E. *Niagara Falls: Icon of the American Sublime*, Cambridge University Press, Cambridge, 1985.

Maclean, Harrison John. *The Fate of the Griffon*, Griffin House, Toronto, 1974.

Maury, Sarah. *An Englishwoman in America*, Thomas Richardson & Sons, London, 1848.

Moore, Christopher: *The Loyalists: Revolution, Exile, Settlement*, Gage Publishing Ltd., Toronto, 1984.

THE NIAGARA FRONTIER

Plato, Earl. *The Neutral Indians (Attawandaron) of Southern Ontario and The Niagara Frontier*; paper, Ft. Erie Historical Museum, 1989.

Radisson, Pierre Esprit. *The Explorations of Pierre Esprit Radisson*. From the original manuscript in the Bodleian Library and the British Museum. Arthur T. Adams, Editor, Loren Kallsen, Modernizer. Ross & Haines, Inc., Minneapolis, 1961.

Read, Colin/**Stagg**, Ronald J. *The Rebellion of 1837 in Upper Canada: A Collection of Documents*; The Champlain Society in cooperation with The Ontario Heritage Foundation, Carleton University Press, Ottawa, 1985.

Rogers, Edward S./**Smith**, Donald B., Editors. *Aboriginal Ontario: Historical Perspectives on the First Nations*; Government of Ontario, Toronto, Oxford, 1994.

Russell, Francis. *The French and Indian Wars*, American Heritage Publishing Co., Inc., New York, 1962.

Tiplin, A. H. *Our Romantic Niagara*, Published by Niagara Falls Heritage Foundation, 1988.

Tovell, Dr. Walter M. *Guide to the Geology of the Niagara Escarpment*; published by The Niagara Escarpment Commission, Georgetown, Ontario, 1992.

THE NIAGARA FRONTIER

Trigger, Bruce, Editor. *Handbook of North American Indians, Northeast*, Volume 15. Smithsonian Institute, Washington, 1978.

Williams, Edward T. *Niagara County, New York, One of the Most Wonderful Regions in the World, A Concise Record of her Progress and People 1821 - 1921*; Published by J.H. Beers & Co., Chicago.

The Canadian Encyclopedia, Second Edition, Hurtig Publishers, Edmonton, 1988.

THE NIAGARA FRONTIER

Index

THE NIAGARA FRONTIER

THE NIAGARA FRONTIER

THE NIAGARA FRONTIER

THE NIAGARA FRONTIER

THE NIAGARA FRONTIER

About the Author

Robert Higgins is a native of Niagara Falls, Ontario, who now lives in Hamilton, Ontario. *The Niagara Frontier: its place in U.S. and Canadian history* is his second book, the first being *The Wreck of the Asia: ships, shoals, storms and a Great Lakes survey*, published by Escart Press in 1995. He also has contributed articles on Domenico Scarlatti, and Tecumseh to various publications. An accomplished athlete, he has competed in long distance running and in short track speed skating. Other interests include cycletouring and photography. Discovering and sharing of the rich and varied history of Ontario and Western New York are his latest pursuits, which includes ongoing research for a third book.

Other Books in the North American Heritage Series

Brannon, Gary (1990). *A Lake to the South of Itasca: Willard Glazier and the Mississippi Fiasco*, 1881-1891, 72p., $9.95, ISBN 0-9692383-2-0

Harding, Les (1991). *The Voyages of Lesser Men: Thumbnail Sketches in Canadian Exploration*, 160p., $16.95, ISBN 0-9692383-5-5

Brannon, Gary (1992). *The Last Voyage of the Tonquin: an Ill-fated expedition to the Pacific northwest*, 97p., $13.95, ISBN 0-9692383-7-1

Harding, Les (1994). *The Journeys of Remarkable Women: their travels on the Canadian frontier*, 147p., $16.95, ISBN 0-9697144-3-2

Higgins, Robert (1995). *The Wreck of the Asia: ships, shoals, storms and a Great Lakes survey*, 100p., $13.95, ISBN 0-9697144-4-0

Higgins, Robert (1996). *The Niagara Frontier: its place in U.S. and Canadian history*, 126p., $16.95, ISBN 0-9681403-0-0

ORDER FROM:

UPNEY EDITIONS
19 Appalachian Crescent
Kitchener, Ontario
N2E 1A3 Canada